Get Started

Preserving

Get Started

Preserving

DK

LONDON, NEW YORK, MUNICH, MELBOURNE, DELHI

Senior Editor Alastair Laing
Project Art Editor Gemma Fletcher
Managing Editor Penny Warren
Managing Art Editor Alison Donovan
Senior Jacket Creative Nicola Powling
Jacket Design Assistant Rosie Levine
Pre-production Producer Sarah Isle
Senior Producers Seyhan Esen, Jen Lockwood
Art Directors Peter Luff, Jane Bull
Publisher Mary Ling

DK Publishing
North American Consultant Kate Curnes
Editor Christy Lusiak
Senior Editor Rebecca Warren

DK India
Editors Kokila Manchanda, Vibha Malhotra
Assistant Art Editors Karan Chaudhary, Tanya Mehrotra
Managing Editor Alka Thakur Hazarika
Deputy Managing Art Editor Priyabrata Roy Chowdhury

Tall Tree Ltd
Editor Joe Fullman
Designer Jonathan Vipond

Written by Susannah Steel,
with additional recipes by Amanda Wright

First American Edition, 2013

Published in the United States by DK Publishing,
375 Hudson Street, New York, New York 10014

13 14 15 16 17   10 9 8 7 6 5 4 3 2 1
001—188214—Jan/2013

Published in Great Britain by Dorling Kindersley Limited.

A catalog record for this book is available from the
Library of Congress.

ISBN 978-1-4654-0194-6

DK books are available at special discounts when purchased in
bulk for sales promotions, premiums, fund-raising, or educational
use. For details, contact: DK Publishing Special Markets, 375
Hudson Street, New York, New York 10014 or
SpecialSales@dk.com.

Printed and bound by Leo Paper Products Ltd, China

Discover more at
www.dk.com

Contents

1
Start Simple

2
Build On It

3
Take It Further

PUBLISHER'S NOTE
The recipes contained in this book have
been created for the ingredients and
techniques indicated. The Publisher is not
responsible for your specific health or
allergy needs that may require supervision.
Nor is the Publisher responsible for any
adverse reactions you may have to the
recipes contained in the book, whether you
follow them as written or modify them to
suit your personal dietary needs or tastes.

Build Your Course

This book divides into broad sections that allow you to build a three-stage course in preserving. All areas are covered, from pickles to potted meats, with recipes that increase in difficulty to develop your skill base and set new challenges as you grow in confidence and experience.

Getting Started

Take your first steps with the preserves in Start Simple, which are easy to master and provide essential foundation skills. In Build On It you will discover many of the classic preserves and, once they are added to your repertoire, you can really call yourself a skilled home preserver. Finally, the recipes in Take It Further feature more unusual and advanced preserving techniques, many with a "wow!" factor that will really stretch your skills and give you a chance to show off.

Tip Boxes Essential pieces of advice are highlighted in pullout boxes that will help you to achieve the best possible results.

Clear photographs of every crucial stage demonstrate how to carry out each preserving technique correctly

Recipe information

Symbols for each recipe highlight the amount of preserve you can expect to make, how long it will take to prepare, and its maxiumum shelf life.

These details feature at the start of each recipe

3 large jars

1½ hours plus straining

12 months

How to **Pages**

Each type of preserve is introduced on "How to" pages, which pinpoint the key techniques to understand before tackling a recipe. Here we explain both the "how?" and the "why?," since understanding the reasons for doing something is crucial to getting it right.

Annotations highlight what to do and how things should look at each step of the recipe

1 After learning about the key techniques, these are then put into practice with an illustrated step-by-step recipe. A visual checklist of ingredients and special equipment, plus a detailed timeline, are included to help you plan.

Useful Advice Recipes are full of tips, reminders, warnings, and advice about what to do if things go wrong—like having a personal tutor helping out in the kitchen.

How to store

At the end of each practice recipe, you will find more information about how and where to store your preserves, how long to leave them until their flavors mature (if applicable), and how long they will keep and how to store them once opened.

Did anything go wrong?

Perfection can be difficult to achieve at the first attempt and here you will also find common problems anticipated, explanations for what probably went wrong, and advice for how to avoid making the same mistake next time.

Try other fruits, vegetables, and flavor combinations

Suggestions for how to vary the recipe the next time you try it by using different fruits or vegetables, or changing additional flavorings such as herbs and spices, are also provided.

Further tips

And look out for additional nuggets of advice, for example on how to select and prepare the best quality produce or how to successfully adapt a basic recipe when preserving different produce.

Now turn over and start preserving! ▶▶▶

Essential **Equipment**

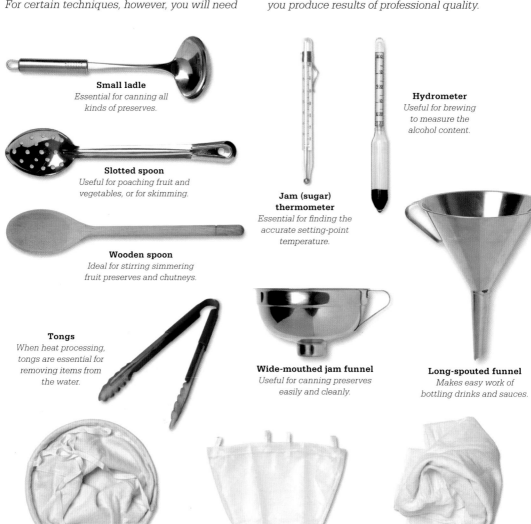

MAKING

Much of the equipment used in preserving is not specialty and can be found in most kitchens. For certain techniques, however, you will need specific tools. Here are the essential items that should meet all your preserving needs, and help you produce results of professional quality.

Small ladle
Essential for canning all kinds of preserves.

Slotted spoon
Useful for poaching fruit and vegetables, or for skimming.

Wooden spoon
Ideal for stirring simmering fruit preserves and chutneys.

Tongs
When heat processing, tongs are essential for removing items from the water.

Jam (sugar) thermometer
Essential for finding the accurate setting-point temperature.

Hydrometer
Useful for brewing to measure the alcohol content.

Wide-mouthed jam funnel
Useful for canning preserves easily and cleanly.

Long-spouted funnel
Makes easy work of bottling drinks and sauces.

Straining bag
For filtering and straining liquids. Particularly useful when brewing.

Jelly bag
Great for straining fruit pulp to make jellies and cordials.

Cheesecloth
Can be used as a strainer, to wrap meats, or to make spice bags.

Food processor
Saves time and effort when mixing, puréeing, mashing, or pulping fruit and vegetables.

Large plastic container with drip tray
Ideal for brining and curing meats, especially large pieces.

Butter mold
For easily making decorative pats of butter.

Demijohn, airlock, and siphon
The essential kit for brewing: for storing the fermenting liquid, sealing, and bottling.

Stainless steel preserving pan
Non-reactive, heavy-bottomed, and wide, this specialty pan is ideal for rapid boiling and making up large quantities.

STORING

Using the right container can make all the difference in preserving. Whether large or small, functional or decorative, glass, earthenware, or freezer-grade plastic, there is a container to suit every preserve. Containers must always be in good condition and sterilized before use (see opposite).

Clear glass bottle
Used with an airtight cork, these are perfect for wines, cider, and cordials.

Ice cube tray
For freezing small portions of herbs.

Plastic freezer containers
Use for freezer jams and for freezing fruit, vegetables, purées, and cooked sauces.

Jam jars
For storing jams, conserves, marmalades, and jellies. Use a new lid, or waxed disc and cellophane cover, every time.

Corks
For stoppering home brews. Ensure they are airtight to prevent oxidization.

Swing stopper bottle
Use for bottling cordials, syrups, and juices.

Ramekin dish
These are the perfect size for potted meats and fish, and for potting up fruit butters, cheese, and jellies.

Specialty preserving jars
Heat-resistant, with non-corrosive lids and replaceable seals, these are specially designed for heat processing (see opposite).

Hygiene and **Food Safety**

Scrupulous hygiene is essential to successful preservation. All equipment and containers must be thoroughly sterilized, and your produce should be of prime quality, kept at the correct temperatures, and consumed within the recommended dates. Any produce showing signs of deterioration should be discarded.

Hygiene Protocol

- Make sure all kitchen surfaces and equipment are completely clean before you start. Remember to use clean cloths and to wash your hands frequently.

- Check that your fridge is clean and set at the correct temperature (40°F/4°C).

- Sterilize all jars, bottles, containers, lids, and equipment that you are using, preferably so that they are ready just before you need them. This ensures that any microbes, which might spoil your preserves, are destroyed.

- Be sure to seal your foods properly before storing. Check on them regularly, use them within date, and throw away any that show signs of deterioration.

- Be extra-careful with meat and fish (raw or cooked). Use the best-quality produce, keep them cold at all times, and separate from other foods. Make sure you use clean equipment at every stage of the process.

Sterilizing Methods

Oven Wash jars, bottles, and lids in hot water, drain, and then dry in a cool oven (275°F/140°C) for 15 minutes.

Dishwasher Put jars, bottles, and lids through a hot wash just before use.

Microwave For non-metal jars. Microwave jars with ¼ cup of water in each for 2 minutes. Drain, then dry on paper towels.

Water bath Put containers in a pan, cover with water, bring slowly to a boil, then turn off the heat. Leave until needed.

Heat Processing

To ensure the saftey of your canned goods, they must be heat processed in a water bath. As the water is heated, any air remaining in the container expands and is released. The seal is then tightened, and a vacuum forms when cool. The container is now completely airtight and its contents protected. If successful, the lid should be sealed firmly in place. For full method and processing times, see pp.116–121.

Essential **Ingredients**

SALT

Salt, or sodium chloride, has long been one of our most important natural preservatives. It works by drawing out the moisture in foods, thus preventing the growth of microorganisms. The higher the concentration of salt, particularly in solutions, the more powerful a preservative it becomes. Salt can be used for preserving vegetables, fish, and meat.

Curing salt
A fine salt designed for curing meat.

Rock salt
Coarse, unrefined rock salt is good for general preserving.

SUGAR

When used in high enough concentrations (60% or higher), sugar is as effective a preservative as salt, and works in a similar way, by drawing the moisture out of foods. It is mostly used for preserving fruit, but can also be used with vinegar to preserve fruit and vegetable mixtures, such as chutneys.

Granulated sugar
A refined sugar with coarse granules. Ideal for general sweet preserves.

Superfine sugar
Finer than granulated and easily dissolved, it is useful for syrups and cordials.

Light brown sugar
The molasses in this sugar can add depth of flavor to chutneys and marmalades.

Jelly sugar
Contains added pectin, for use with low-pectin fruits to help them set.

FATS

Although not preserving agents, oils and animal fats have a useful role in preserving. Used to cover already processed foods, they form a seal protecting the produce from airborne microorganisms. Blanched and dried vegetables and potted meats can be protected by fats.

Butter
Butter is clarified and then used to seal potted meats.

Goose fat
Used for sealing potted meats as an alternative to lard.

Olive oil
Its delicious fruity flavor makes it the ideal oil for preserving.

Sunflower oil
An oil with a lighter, more subtle flavor.

VINEGARS

Another important preserving agent of long-standing, vinegar is made by fermenting alcohol to produce acetic acid. Provided its acid content is 5% or higher, vinegar will prevent the growth of most microorganisms, including e-coli, which cause food to deteriorate. It is mostly used to preserve vegetables as pickles, relishes, and sauces, and also oily fish.

Malt vinegar
This strong brown vinegar is suitable for savory preserves with robust flavors.

Pickling and spirit vinegar
Pickling vinegar can be bought ready-spiced, or homemade from spirit vinegar (see p57).

Red wine vinegar
Fermented from red wine, this vinegar can be used for added color and flavor.

White wine vinegar
Fermented from white wine, this vinegar has a lighter, more delicate flavor than red.

Cider vinegar
Fermented from cider, this vinegar has a subtle flavor of apples.

LEMONS

Lemons can be invaluable when making jams and jellies. When using fruits with a low-pectin content, adding lemon juice draws out the pectin, helping the mixture to set.

The acid in lemon juice also helps prevent the sugar in sweet preserves from crystallizing.

SPICES AND FLAVORING

Adding herbs and spices can hugely enhance your preserves. Not only do they add wonderful flavors and aromas, but many can aid digestion and even actively help the preserving process.

Ground spices
Whenever possible, grind whole spices just before use; once ground, they can quickly lose their flavors and aromas.

Herbs
Fresh or dried herbs will enhance the flavors of pickles, relishes, and vegetables in oil. They can also be used to flavor jellies for classic accompaniments to roasted meats.

Whole spices
Whole spices will keep for up to two years in an airtight container. Most often used for flavoring vinegar, they can be left in the jar or tied in a cheesecloth bag and removed before canning (see p.57).

The science of **How Foods Spoil**

Microorganisms such as fungi, yeasts, and bacteria are present in all living things, in the atmosphere, and on the surface of food. In moist, warm, airy, alkaline conditions these microorganisms thrive, causing foods to deteriorate and spoil. Enzymes are organic catalysts present in plant and animal cells that contribute to the rate at which foods spoil.

Enzymes are naturally occurring proteins in food that speed up, or catalyze, the chemical reactions caused by microorganisms that change the appearance, texture, and taste of food. However, enzymes are fragile: they can be destroyed by very high heat or slowed down by very cold temperatures.

Enzymes help convert one set of molecules into different molecules through a chemical reaction

Diagram of enzyme action

Different enzymes are designed to work on or "fit" specific molecules

Enzyme latches on to molecules to catalyze them

Products are released

Enzyme is ready to catalyze further molecules

Bacteria In the right conditions, single-celled bacteria will multiply rapidly and cause food to decay. For example, they can turn warm, unsterilized milk sour in a matter of hours. Some bacteria can also cause food poisoning, so care must always be taken when preserving meat, fish, or vegetables under oil.

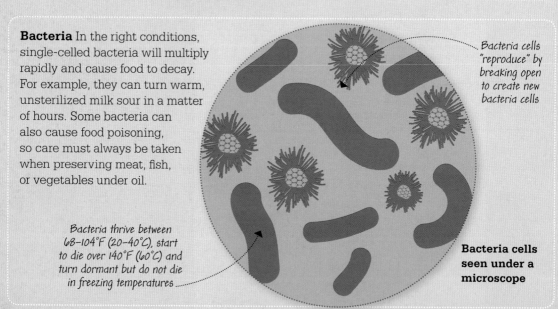

Bacteria cells "reproduce" by breaking open to create new bacteria cells

Bacteria thrive between 68–104°F (20–40°C), start to die over 140°F (60°C) and turn dormant but do not die in freezing temperatures

Bacteria cells seen under a microscope

Molds are microscopic fungi that live on moist foods in warm, humid conditions. Most are threadlike organisms with roots, or rhizoids, that grow down into a food source, and fruiting bodies that rise up with spores at the tip. The spores, which give a mold its color, are released when dry to float through the air to form new molds. While a few molds are beneficial—in cheesemaking, for example— others will cause foods to rot, and can release harmful toxins.

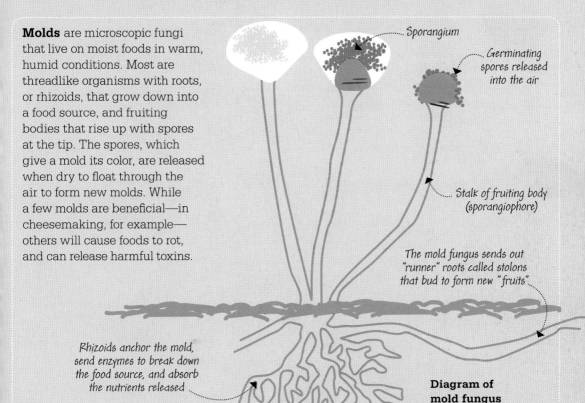

Sporangium

Germinating spores released into the air

Stalk of fruiting body (sporangiophore)

The mold fungus sends out "runner" roots called stolons that bud to form new "fruits"

Rhizoids anchor the mold, send enzymes to break down the food source, and absorb the nutrients released

Diagram of mold fungus

Yeast Part of the fungi group of organisms, single-celled yeasts prefer warm, moist, slightly acidic environments. Like mold, yeasts secrete enzymes that break down organic matter into nutrients they can absorb. Some yeasts are useful, breaking down, or "fermenting," sugars to produce alcohol and carbon dioxide, which also causes bread to rise. Other yeasts spoil food and cause disease.

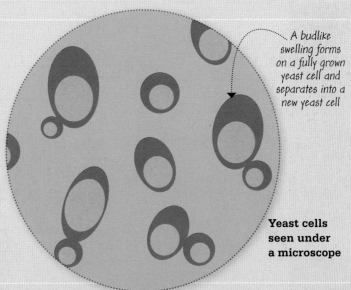

A budlike swelling forms on a fully grown yeast cell and separates into a new yeast cell

Yeast cells seen under a microscope

The science of **How To Preserve**

The aim of preserving is to slow down the activity of microorganisms and enzymes or destroy them altogether; they cannot survive in acidic or dry conditions, in high concentrations of salt and sugar, in alcohol, or in high temperatures. A preserve will often employ different techniques, for example jams combine heat with a high concentration of sugar.

Freeze The colder a food is, the slower its rate of deterioration. Bacterial action reduces with refrigeration, while freezing stops it altogether; enzyme activity, however, is only slowed down. Vegetables must be blanched in boiling water first to destroy enzymes and microorganisms, while herbs can be mixed with oil and fruit should be sprinkled with sugar to limit enzyme activity while frozen.

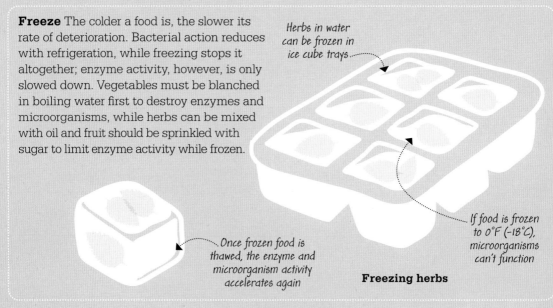

Herbs in water can be frozen in ice cube trays

If food is frozen to 0°F (–18°C), microorganisms can't function

Once frozen food is thawed, the enzyme and microorganism activity accelerates again

Freezing herbs

Heat Boiling or blanching food at high temperatures destroys all enzyme activity and almost all microorganisms. The more acidic the food, such as fruit, the more easily microorganisms are destroyed by heat. Boiled preserves must be sealed in airless conditions (e.g. airtight jars) to prolong their shelf life.

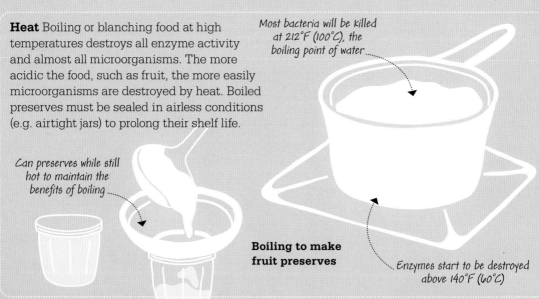

Most bacteria will be killed at 212°F (100°C), the boiling point of water

Can preserves while still hot to maintain the benefits of boiling

Boiling to make fruit preserves

Enzymes start to be destroyed above 140°F (60°C)

Use strong concentrations

Alcohol, acid, and salt and sugar in high concentrations all create environments that prevent the growth of microorganisms or, in the case of alcohol, destroy them completely. Naturally acidic fruit is usually preserved in a concentrated sugar solution or alcohol. Vegetables, which are more alkaline, are preserved in acidic vinegar or a salt solution, or a combination of both.

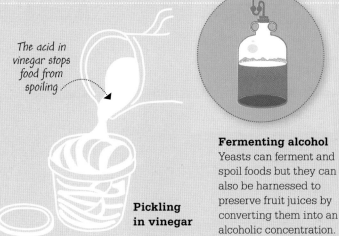

The acid in vinegar stops food from spoiling

Pickling in vinegar

Fermenting alcohol

Yeasts can ferment and spoil foods but they can also be harnessed to preserve fruit juices by converting them into an alcoholic concentration.

Exclude air

A seal of fat or oil can prevent any airborne microorganisms from coming into contact with food and spoiling it. It also starves aerobic bacteria present in food of oxygen, which it requires to survive and increase. Heat processing jars and bottles of preserves prolongs shelf life by forcing air to escape as steam to leave a sterile vacuum.

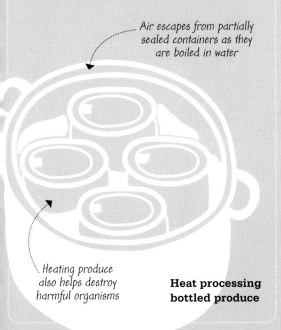

Air escapes from partially sealed containers as they are boiled in water

Heating produce also helps destroy harmful organisms

Heat processing bottled produce

Remove moisture

Microorganisms need moisture to grow, and die off in dry conditions. Food can be dried using warm air or an oven, or sealed in a concentrated solution of salt or sugar that draws out moisture by osmosis.

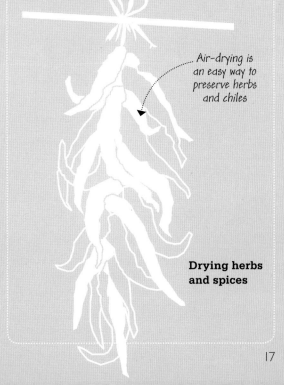

Air-drying is an easy way to preserve herbs and chiles

Drying herbs and spices

1

Start Simple

The preserving techniques in this section are easy to master and provide numerous simple ways of capturing the flavors of fresh produce. Choose from a variety of methods, from freezing and bottling to basic jams, pickles, and relishes.

In this section, learn to prepare or make:

Frozen Fruit
pp.20–23

Freezer Jam
pp.24–27

Frozen Veg
pp.28–31

Frozen Herbs
pp.32–33

Pesto
pp.34–41

Vegetables in Oil
pp.42–45

Fruits in Alcohol
pp.46–51

Preserves in Salt *pp.52–55*

Pickles
pp.56–61

Freezer Pickles
pp.62–63

Chutney
pp.64–71

Relish
pp.72–75

How to **Freeze Fresh Fruit**

Freezing is a wonderfully easy way of dramatically slowing down the deterioration of fruit and keeping as much of its flavor and nutrients as possible. It is best to freeze fruit with sugar, as this helps it to retain its texture when thawed. Some fruits can simply be frozen whole, while others need a little basic preparation.

The fruit should be coated in sugar

Open freezing prevents fruit from clumping together

Use small freezer bags

Open-freeze with sugar

Fresh fruits need to be frozen individually first—a procedure called open-freezing (see p.14)—to prevent them from squishing together. Arrange the fruits in a single layer on a baking sheet, sprinkle with granulated sugar, and put the sheet in the freezer.

Pack into freezer bags

It will probably take an hour or so for the fruits to freeze. Once they are completely frozen, remove the sheet and pack the fruits into freezer bags, preferably portion-sized freezer bags so you can defrost just a little at a time, as required.

Tip Remove any pits from fruit and cut larger fruit in half or into slices before freezing. Juicy fruit like peaches can be puréed with a little sugar and lemon juice, and frozen in freezer jars. Be sure to leave a small gap at the top of the jar for the purée to expand.

Sugar firms the skins of the fruits as they freeze, helping them retain their shape while frozen and once thawed

Only freeze produce that is in good condition

Label and date

Write a "best before" date on each bag. All fruits start spoiling after a certain period in the freezer, so check the table (see p.22) to see how long it can be stored. Freezing breaks down the fruit's cell walls, so it will be squishy when defrosted, but still tasty.

Freezing Times for Fresh Fruit

This table lists the most suitable raw fruits for freezing, the various
ways in which you can freeze them, and their maximum storage
times. These times are appropriate only if you freeze the fruits below
0°F (–18°C). Aim to use them well before these time limits, however, and
leave them to thaw in the fridge before using.

Fruits	Freezing Times		
	Sprinkle with sugar and open-freeze on baking sheets (see pp.20–21) (months)	Pack in freezer jars, cover in syrup (see p.116) or sugar, and freeze (months)	Purée, pack in freezer jars, and freeze (months)
Apples	9	9	N/A
Apricots (ripe)	9	9	6
Blackberries	12	12	6
Black currants	12	12	6
Blueberries	12	12	6
Cherries	6	6	6
Citrus fruits	6	N/A	N/A
Cranberries	12	12	6
Figs	9	9	6
Gooseberries	12	12	6
Loganberries	12	12	6
Melons	9	9	6
Nectarines	9	9	6
Peaches	9	9	6
Plums	9	9	6
Raspberries	12	12	6
Rhubarb	12	12	N/A
Strawberries	9	9	6
Fruit syrups (pp.110–111)	Pour into freezer jars and freeze for 9 months		

Remove the **apricot** pits and cut into halves or slices

Strip the **currants** from their stems first before open-freezing them

Cut **plums** in half and remove their pits before freezing

Peaches are best frozen in jars as a purée, as the freezing process effectively purées them anyway

Raspberries are an excellent fruit to open-freeze whole

Apples must be peeled, sliced, and dipped in lemon juice first to prevent any discoloration

Open-freezing is the best way to freeze **cranberries**—you can use them straight from the freezer without thawing first

23

How to **Make Freezer Jam**

If you find traditional jams too sweet, or you have very ripe, juicy fruits that would be hard to set as jam, try making freezer jam—a sweetened, uncooked purée thickened with agar, a natural Japanese gelling agent, and frozen to a jelly-like set to preserve its nutrients and flavor. The process is simple and quick, and the results taste refreshing and flavorful.

Tip Use 1lb 2oz (500g) total weight of fresh fruits with 1 tablespoon each of agar and lemon juice and ¼–⅔ cup of sugar, depending on how sweet you like your freezer jam.

A coarse purée will retain the texture of the fruit

Squeeze lemon juice straight into the purée

Agar is made from seaweed, and so is suitable for vegetarians and vegans

Purée the fruit

To prepare the fruit, wash it only if necessary. Put it in a bowl and crush gently with the back of a fork to make a coarse, rather than a smooth, purée. You can mix in a tablespoon of lemon juice, which is about half a fresh lemon, for added flavor, if you like.

Dissolve agar and sugar

Sprinkle the agar into a small saucepan of water and leave for 2–3 minutes to soften. Bring slowly to a boil without stirring, and simmer for 3–5 minutes. Stir until the agar has dissolved, then add the sugar. Keep stirring for 2–3 minutes until the sugar has dissolved.

Keep stirring the
purée as you pour
in the agar syrup

Leave a gap of
½in (1cm) at the top of
each container to
allow the jam to
expand as it freezes

Combine the ingredients

Pour the hot syrup into the bowl of puréed
fruit, stirring constantly with a wooden
spoon to combine the ingredients
thoroughly. It's worth using a spatula to
scrape the last of the syrup from the pan into
the fruit mixture to ensure the best set.

Pour into freezer containers

The jam thickens rapidly as it cools, so pour it
into clean, portion-sized freezer containers
before it starts to solidify. Allow the jam to cool
in the fridge overnight before sealing and
freezing. To use the jam, thaw, refrigerate, and
add to yogurt or desserts, or spread on bread.

Blueberry and Raspberry Freezer Jam

1lb 2oz (500g)　　15 minutes　　6 months

Ingredients

8oz (225g) blueberries

8oz (225g) raspberries

2 tsp lemon juice

1 tbsp agar flakes or 1 tsp agar powder

½ cup granulated sugar

CRUSH THE FRUIT

Bring the blueberries and raspberries to room temperature so they release their juices properly and are soft enough to be crushed gently. Then put them in a bowl with the lemon juice and crush coarsely with the back of a fork or a potato masher.

Careful! You want to produce a coarse purée with plenty of juicy chunks to enjoy.

PREPARE THE AGAR

Sprinkle the agar over ¾ cup of water in a small saucepan. Allow the agar to soften for 2–3 minutes before heating the mix gently over low heat until it comes to the boil. Simmer gently for 3–5 minutes.

Tip Avoid stirring the agar with a spoon while it softens, as this might prevent it from absorbing the water. Instead, agitate the mix by giving the pan a quick swirl just before heating it. Once the mix is boiling, stir it occasionally to make sure the agar has dissolved.

Add the sugar and continue to stir over low heat for 2–3 minutes until it has completely dissolved: look for any sugar crystals as you stir, just to be sure. Remove the pan from the heat.

MIX THE SYRUP AND THE FRUIT

Pour the agar syrup into the bowl of crushed berries. Stir constantly but gently to combine.

CAN THE JAM

Pour the jam into clean, portion-sized freezer containers. Allow at least ½in (1cm) of space at the top. Let cool, then seal, label, and refrigerate overnight before freezing. To use, thaw in the fridge overnight first, then keep refrigerated and consume within 2 weeks.

Strawberry Freezer Jam

1lb 5oz (600g)   **15 minutes**   **6 months**

Ingredients

1lb 2oz (500g) strawberries, washed only
if necessary

1 tsp lemon juice

1 tbsp agar flakes or 1 tsp agar powder

¼–½ cup granulated sugar

CRUSH THE FRUIT

Roughly crush the strawberries in a bowl
with the lemon juice using the back of a fork or
a potato masher.

Careful! Avoid crushing the fruit too fiercely.

PREPARE THE AGAR

Sprinkle the agar over ¾ cup of water in a small
saucepan. Allow the agar to soften for 2–3 minutes
before heating gently over low heat until it comes
to a boil. Simmer gently for 3–5 minutes.

Tip Stirring the agar as it softens may prevent
it from absorbing the water. Instead, just give the
pan a quick swirl before heating, to agitate the
mix. Once the mix is boiling, stir it occasionally
until the agar dissolves.

Add the sugar and continue to stir over low
heat for 2–3 minutes until it has all dissolved and
you can't see any more sugar crystals in the
solution. Remove the pan from the heat.

MIX THE SYRUP AND THE FRUIT

Pour the agar syrup into the bowl of crushed
strawberries. Stir constantly but gently to combine.

CAN THE JAM

Pour the jam into clean, portion-sized freezer
containers. Allow at least ½in (1cm) of space at the
top. Let cool, then seal, label, refrigerate overnight
to thicken fully, and freeze. To use, thaw in the
fridge overnight first, then keep refrigerated and
consume within 2 weeks.

How to **Freeze Blanched Vegetables**

Freezing is one of the most convenient ways to preserve vegetables, and the results are worth it: thawed frozen produce tastes almost as fresh as it does when picked. Some vegetables need to be blanched (briefly cooked in water) before freezing to destroy the enzymes that can cause their color, flavor, and texture to deteriorate.

Keep the water at a rolling boil as you add the vegetables

Iced water is better than just ice as it provides all-over contact for faster chilling

The vegetables will stop cooking in the iced water

Blanch the vegetables

Boil a pan of lightly salted water and add a small handful of vegetables. Bring quickly back to a boil, and cook the vegetables for 2–3 minutes. Cook the vegetables in small batches, so the water boils soon after the vegetables have been added. Repeat until all vegetables are done.

Ice and drain

Transfer each batch of vegetables immediately to a bowl of iced water to halt the cooking process. Then drain the vegetables and pat them dry with paper towels. Dry the vegetables thoroughly before freezing; the firmer and less watery their texture, the better they will freeze.

Freeze in different-sized portions, depending on how they will be used

Tip Only freeze or open-freeze the produce once it has cooled completely after the blanching process.

Green beans can be cooked straight from frozen

Pack into freezer bags

When the vegetables are dry, pack them in convenient portions in freezer bags or containers. If you want to freeze larger batches, open-freeze them first (see p.14) to keep them from sticking together and then store them in large freezer bags.

29

Freezing Times for Blanched Vegetables

This table lists the most suitable vegetables for freezing, how to prepare them, how long to blanch them for, and their maximum storage times. However, you should aim to use the produce well before these time limits. Ensure that you freeze all produce below 0°F (−18°C). All these vegetables, apart from sweet corn cobs, can be cooked straight from the freezer.

Vegetables	How to prepare	Blanch (minutes)	Freeze (months)
Asparagus	Trim	2–4	9
Beans, baby green	Leave whole	2–3	9
Beans, fava	Pod	2–3	12
Beans, large green (tender)	Slice	2	9
Broccoli florets	Separate	2	9
Brussels sprouts	Leave whole	3	9
Cabbages	Slice	2	6
Carrots (small)	Leave whole	5	9
Carrots	Slice	2–3	9
Cauliflower florets	Separate	3	6
Fennel	Slice	2	6
Globe artichokes (bottoms)	Leave whole	4	9
Globe artichokes (baby)	Leave whole	3	9
Parsnips	Peel, chop	2–3	9
Peas	Pod	1–2	12
Romanesco broccoli florets	Separate	2	9
Snow peas	Leave whole	1	9
Spinach	Wash	1	9
Sugarsnap peas	Leave whole	2	9
Sweet corn (cobs)	Leave whole	6	12
Sweet corn (kernels)	Separate	2	12
Swiss chard (leaves/stalks)	Wash, chop	1–2	9

Trim the ends,
slice, blanch, and
open-freeze
large green beans
before storing them
in the freezer

Scrubbed **carrots**
are best sliced in
matchsticks or
rounds before being
blanched and frozen

Cut **romanesco
and cauliflower**
into small florets
before blanching
and freezing

Fava beans store
very well after
open-freezing,
retaining all their
texture

Blanch **spinach**
briefly and then
squeeze gently to
remove the moisture
before packing into
freezer bags

Blanch and freeze whole
sweet corn cobs, or stand the
cobs upright, run a sharp knife
down the sides to strip off the
kernels, and blanch the kernels
before freezing

How to **Freeze Herbs**

Preserving delicate herbs by freezing them guarantees you can always include their fresh, fragrant flavors, essential oils, and colors in dishes. However, the freezing process does affect their texture, so they are best frozen in oil or water for ease of use. Add them in the same quantities as fresh herbs—they are not concentrated in flavor like dried herbs.

Preserve in oil

Drizzle in olive oil to coat the herbs lightly

CHOP AND ADD OIL
Fresh herb leaves become limp when frozen, so strip them from their stems, put in a food processor, and pulse until finely chopped. Add 1 tablespoon of extra virgin olive oil for every 3 tablespoons of chopped herbs.

PACK INTO FREEZER BAGS
Divide the chopped herb mixture into batches and spoon each batch into very small freezer bags. Herbs in oil freeze well for up to 4 months. Good herbs to preserve in oil include basil, parsley, and cilantro.

Preserve in water

Chop the leaves so they are easier to handle when defrosted

CHOP FINELY

Ice-cube trays provide an excellent way to freeze herbs such as chives, parsley, tarragon, dill, chervil, and cilantro. Strip the leaves from their stems and pulse briefly in a food processor. Alternatively, you could finely chop the herbs by hand.

Tip Frozen herbs work well in salad dressings, hot dishes, sauces, stuffings, and toppings. If you make frozen ice cubes, you can pop them straight from the freezer into pans of hot food. Use the ice cubes within 6 months.

Each ice cube contains about 1 tablespoon of chopped herbs

FILL THE TRAY

Fill each ice-cube hole up to the brim with chopped herbs and pour in just enough water to cover. Put the tray in the freezer for about 2 hours, or until the herb cubes have frozen, then remove them from the tray and divide into small freezer bags.

How to **Make Pesto**

Pesto is an intensely flavored paste of ground aromatic herbs
or strong spices, combined with oil and a strong cheese such as
Parmesan. Pesto is not a long-lasting preserve because it contains no
significant levels of salt, vinegar, or sugar, but sealing it with a layer
of oil to exclude the air will allow you to store it for up to 2 weeks.

Tip Add just enough
olive oil to give you the
desired consistency.
Don't be afraid to add a
little extra oil, if you like
a more fluid pesto, or less,
if you want it firmer.

*Pour in just
enough oil to make
a glistening paste*

Using a food processor

The quickest and least laborious way to make
pesto is in a food processor. You can quickly
blend all the dry ingredients and add the oil
while the processor is still running to create
a smooth, fine-textured paste. However, be
sure not to add too much oil at once.

Press the pestle down firmly and stir it around the mortar

Pound the basil, toasted pine nuts, and garlic first, before adding the cheese

Use a wooden spoon to stir in the oil

You can adjust the consistency of the paste to your liking

Drizzle in the olive oil a little at a time

By hand

Pesto can also be made in a pestle and mortar, although it requires a lot of elbow grease! It gives the pesto a more robust texture and allows you more time to judge the amount of oil needed to bind the mixture to your desired consistency. Season to taste and serve.

Basil Pesto

A traditional pesto that derives from Genoa, Italy, this pungently flavored condiment made with fresh basil leaves is extremely easy to make, and very quick if you own a food processor. It tastes divine simply tossed with pasta or added to crushed new potatoes.

1 small jar

 Approx. 10–15 minutes

 **2 weeks (2 months, if frozen)**

Ingredients

scant 1oz (25g) pine nuts

2oz (60g) basil leaves

1 large clove garlic, peeled

1½oz (45g) Parmesan cheese, finely grated

⅓ cup extra virgin olive oil,
    plus extra for sealing the pesto

sea salt

freshly ground black pepper

Equipment

frying pan

wooden spoon

food processor or mortar and pestle

airtight jar with lid

pine nuts

basil leaves

garlic clove

Parmesan cheese

extra virgin olive oil

sea salt

black pepper

frying pan

wooden spoon

food processor

airtight jar with lid

1 Dry fry the pine nuts in a clean frying pan and cook over low heat for 2–3 minutes, stirring frequently until just toasted but not colored. Remove from the heat.

Careful! Nuts can burn very quickly. Keep the heat low, keep stirring, and don't leave them unattended. Dry-frying pine nuts helps to release their flavor, but if allowed to color they will lose their creaminess when processed.

Wash and gently dry the basil leaves, if needed, before chopping them

2 Place the pine nuts, basil, and garlic in a food processor and blend until almost smooth. Alternatively, use a pestle and mortar (see p.35).

Tip Use a spatula intermittently to scrape down the sides of the processor so all the ingredients are evenly processed.

3 Add the Parmesan cheese to the processor. Keep it running and slowly add the extra virgin olive oil through the feed tube until it is all incorporated.

Help! Don't worry about over-working the ingredients while you keep the processor running. The flavor of the pesto won't suffer from being finely blended.

Drizzle the olive oil gradually into the processor so it combines well with the other ingredients

Use a little more olive oil to seal the pesto

The pesto should be a glistening paste once all the oil has been added

4 Season the pesto to taste and then spoon it into a warm, sterilized, airtight jar. Pour a thin layer of olive oil over the top of the pesto to seal it.

Remember The layer of oil on top of the pesto prevents any exposure to air inside the jar. Make sure all the pesto is completely submerged beneath the oil.

How to store

You can store the pesto in the fridge for up to 2 weeks.

If you make a lot of pesto, you can freeze it in small freezer containers or ice-cube trays for up to 2 months. Just remember to leave out the Parmesan cheese from the ingredients, because it loses its flavor when frozen. Before serving, defrost the pesto and stir in the required quantity of grated Parmesan cheese.

Did anything go wrong?

The basil in the pesto discolored. It has been exposed to the air too long and oxidized.

Next time, be sure to store the fresh pesto in an airtight container and cover completely with oil. This prevents the pesto from getting oxidized.

Use only very fresh herbs, making sure you discard any stems or leaves that are tinged brown.

Other combinations

The Italian word "pesto" roughly translates as "pounded" and does not refer to any one recipe. There are plenty of variations of pesto you could try. Parsley and walnuts go well together, as do arugula, basil, parsley, and chives with cashew nuts, while wild garlic leaves and pine nuts make a fabulous seasonal combination.

Try more Pesto recipes ▶ ▶ ▶

Cilantro and Walnut Pesto

1 small jar **10 minutes** **2 weeks, refrigerated**

Ingredients

approx. 1oz (30g) bunch of fresh cilantro

1 large garlic clove, peeled

1oz (30g) walnut pieces

a good grinding of black pepper

a good pinch of salt

1oz (30g) Parmesan cheese, freshly grated

5 tbsp extra virgin olive oil

PROCESS THE INGREDIENTS

Trim the stems from the cilantro and lightly crush the garlic clove by pressing it under the side of the blade of a large chopping knife. Put the cilantro leaves in a food processor with the other ingredients and 1 tablespoon of the oil and purée for a few seconds.

Remember If you prefer a coarser paste, you can make the pesto in a pestle and mortar (see p.35).

ADD THE OIL

Gradually add the remaining oil while keeping the food processor running until the ingredients form a glistening paste.

CAN IN A JAR

Spoon the pesto into a sterilized jar, making sure you don't leave any air pockets, and pour a little oil over the surface to exclude any air. Seal, label, and store in the fridge.

Remember It's important to cover the pesto surface completely with oil to keep out airborne microbes and to starve any microbes in the pesto of air. If you don't use up all the pesto for one meal, cover what is left in the jar with about a tablespoon or so of olive oil and screw the lid back on tightly.

Arugula Pesto

1 small jar   **15 minutes**   **2 weeks, refrigerated**

Ingredients

1oz (30g) arugula, washed

1 garlic clove, peeled

1oz (30g) blue cheese, crumbled or diced, depending on the texture

1½oz (45g) blanched, toasted almonds

4 tbsp extra virgin olive oil

salt and freshly ground black pepper

PROCESS THE INGREDIENTS

Put the arugula in a food processor and lightly crush the garlic clove by pressing it under the side of a large chopping knife. Add the garlic, cheese, almonds, and 2 tablespoons of the oil to the food processor and purée for a few seconds.

Remember You can make the pesto in a pestle and mortar for a coarser texture (see p.35).

ADD THE OIL

Gradually add the remaining oil while keeping the food processor running until the ingredients form a glistening paste. Season to taste with salt and freshly ground pepper.

CAN IN A JAR

Spoon the pesto into a sterilized jar, making sure you don't leave any air pockets, and pour a little oil over the surface to exclude any air. Seal, label, and store in the fridge.

Remember It's important to cover the surface of the pesto completely with oil to keep out airborne microbes and to starve any microbes in the pesto of air. If you don't use up all the pesto for one meal, cover what is left over with about a tablespoon or so of olive oil and screw the lid back on tightly.

How to **Prepare Vegetables in Oil**

Oil is not a preservative but an air excluder, or sealant, protecting the produce against airborne microbes and starving aerobic bacteria. It also brings out the flavor of many vegetables, so it is worth storing fresh produce in oil for short periods of time. However, it is important to process the vegetables first, to kill any microorganisms that may otherwise survive.

Acidify the vegetables

Boil the chopped vegetables with sugar, salt, and just enough vinegar to cover them until soft on the outside but very firm in the center. The acid in vinegar prevents the growth of most microbes. Heating destroys microbes and the enzymes that trigger deterioration.

Pour in the oil

Pour enough olive oil into the jars to cover the vegetables, to prevent the air from coming into contact with the food. The oil starves aerobic bacteria of the oxygen they need to survive. Press the vegetables down gently to expel any trapped air pockets.

Italian-style Vegetables

2 medium jars | **30 minutes, plus 1 week** | **1–2 months, refrigerated**

Ingredients

1lb 5oz (600g) mixed seasonal vegetables

about 2 cups white wine vinegar

2 tsp granulated sugar

2 tsp sea salt

approx. $^2/_3$ cup extra virgin olive oil

seasonings (dried fennel seeds, dried oregano, bay leaf, rosemary, lemon thyme, chile flakes)

CHOP THE VEGETABLES

Wash and peel the vegetables, if necessary, and slice each into evenly sized pieces about ½in (1cm) thick.

Tip Chop vegetables such as eggplant, fennel, small florets of cauliflower or broccoli, zucchini, celery, carrots, green beans, and peppers. Leave small shallots and mushrooms whole.

BLANCH IN VINEGAR

Put a small batch of the sliced vegetables in a stainless-steel saucepan and pour in just enough vinegar to cover. Add the sugar and salt and bring to a boil.

Boil the vegetable slices in batches until *al dente* (soft on the outside but firm in the center): about 2–3 minutes for tender vegetables and 5–10 minutes for firmer ones. To test, cool a piece of vegetable under water before trying it with your teeth, pinching it between two fingers, or cutting it in half with a knife. Then remove the vegetables from the pan with a slotted spoon, pat dry with paper towels, and let cool. Repeat this process with the remaining vegetables.

PACK INTO JARS

Pack the vegetables into sterilized jars and add some seasonings. Choose from 1 teaspoon dried fennel seeds, 1 teaspoon dried oregano, 1 fresh or dried bay leaf, 1 sprig rosemary, 1 sprig lemon thyme, or a pinch of chile flakes. Cover with olive oil and tap the jars lightly on a work surface to remove any air bubbles. Add more oil to cover completely. Seal and label the jars, and store in the fridge. Leave for at least 1 week before opening to allow the flavors to develop. Add more oil as needed so the vegetables are always covered.

Careful! Make sure the surfaces of the vegetables are not exposed to the air to keep out airborne microbes.

Mixed Peppers in Oil

2 medium jars   **40 minutes**   **3–4 weeks, refrigerated**

Ingredients

3 red bell peppers

3 orange bell peppers

3 yellow bell peppers

1 tsp dried oregano

sea salt

freshly ground black pepper

2 tbsp extra virgin olive oil, plus extra to cover

2 tbsp cider vinegar

ROAST THE PEPPERS

Preheat the oven to 400°F (200°C). Arrange the peppers in a roasting pan and roast in the oven for 20–30 minutes until they are lightly charred—the skin will pucker up from the flesh and start to burn in patches. Immediately, while the peppers are still hot, place them inside sandwich or freezer bags. Tie the bags closed and allow the peppers to cool.

Why? The steam trapped inside the bags will help loosen the skins and make the peppers easier to peel.

PREPARE THE PEPPERS

Cut the peppers in half and scrape out the seeds. Now remove the skin and any stems.

Slice the flesh into wide strips, then place in a bowl, and add the oregano, salt, and black pepper. Mix the oil and vinegar together, pour it into the bowl, and combine with the peppers.

CAN IN JARS

Spoon the peppers into sterilized jars and pour in the juices from the bowl. Add enough olive oil to cover the peppers completely. Seal and label the jars, and refrigerate. Add more oil as needed, making sure the vegetables are always covered. Use within 1 month.

Artichokes in Oil

1 small jar   **45 minutes**   **2 months, refrigerated**

Ingredients

10 baby artichokes

1¼ cups white wine vinegar

1 tbsp sea salt

thyme sprigs (optional)

For the marinade

2 cups extra virgin olive oil

⅓ cup white wine vinegar

handful of black peppercorns

PREPARE THE ARTICHOKES

Trim the stems of the artichokes and remove the outer leaves (about 5–6 layers), leaving the paler, more tender leaves. Trim off about 1in (2.5cm) from the tops and discard. The fuzzy, silky mass of immature florets at the center of the artichoke is known as the "choke" and is unpleasant to eat. Remove the choke to expose the succulent heart beneath. Leave whole or cut in half.

BLANCH THE ARTICHOKES

Put the vinegar and salt in a preserving pan or heavy-bottomed stainless-steel saucepan. Add 1¼ cups of water and bring to a boil. Add the artichokes and simmer for 3–5 minutes until *al dente*. Drain, let cool, and cut lengthwise into quarters.

Remember The acid in the vinegar prevents the growth of most microbes. Heating also destroys microbes and the enzymes that trigger deterioration.

PREPARE THE MARINADE

Place the marinade ingredients in a pan and bring to a boil. Add the artichokes to the mix. Bring back to a boil, then turn off the heat. Allow the artichokes to cool in the marinade.

PACK INTO JARS

Put the artichokes into a sterilized jar with a non-metallic or vinegar-proof lid. Add the thyme sprigs, if you are using them. Pour in all the marinade to cover the vegetables completely. Seal and label the jars, and refrigerate.

Careful! As you consume the artichokes, keep adding more oil to the jar as needed to ensure the artichokes are not exposed to the air. Use within 2 months.

How to **Bottle Fruits in Alcohol**

Fresh fruits bottled in alcohol are possibly the easiest preserves to prepare and will keep almost indefinitely, as no microorganisms can grow in high concentrations of alcohol. The combination of succulent, sweet fruit and alcohol, such as brandy, rum, whiskey, vodka, or gin, makes for one of the most delicious and indulgent of treats.

Bottling in cold alcohol

Almost all fruits can be preserved in alcohol, and the results are often better than freezing

Tip This method is best for thin-skinned fruits like berries, plums, and cherries. Prick thicker-skinned fruits with a darning needle to let the alcohol infuse the fruit.

When the sugar has dissolved the liquid will be completely clear

ADD SUGAR AND ALCOHOL
Gently pack the fresh fruit into a wide-necked sterilized preserving jar without bruising or squishing them. Add enough sugar to fill one-third of the jar and then pour in enough alcohol to completely cover the fruit.

DISSOLVE THE SUGAR
Tap the jar lightly on the work surface to expel any air bubbles, and then seal the jar. The sugar will gradually dissolve in the alcohol, but give the jar an occasional shake to help it dissolve completely.

Combining with hot syrup

You can adjust the sugar content in the syrup to taste, depending on how tart the fruit is

MAKE A SUGAR SYRUP

Put cold water in a large saucepan, add sugar (½–1¼ cups per 2 cups total liquid), and heat gently, stirring continuously until all the sugar crystals have dissolved. Bring to a boil and simmer for 5 minutes. Submerge the fruit in the syrup and return to a boil.

Tie the spice bag with a long piece of string so it's easier to remove

POACH THE FRUIT AND FLAVOR THE SYRUP

Reduce the heat and briefly poach the fruit according to the recipe. Lift out the fruit with a slotted spoon and let cool. You can flavor the syrup after poaching by adding a cheesecloth spice bag of whole spices (see p.57). Bring the syrup back to a boil and boil rapidly for a few minutes. Allow to cool slightly before adding to the jar and topping up with the alcohol.

Apricots and Almonds in Amaretto

1 large jar

20 minutes, plus 4 weeks

12 months

Ingredients

⅓ cup granulated sugar

1lb (450g) apricots, halved and pitted

2oz (60g) blanched almonds

approx. 1 cup amaretto

Tip If you prefer to peel the apricots before canning them, plunge the whole fruits into a bowl of boiling water for 1 minute, then a bowl of cold water, and peel off the skins (see p.28).

MAKE THE SYRUP

Heat the sugar and ⅔ cup water in a large saucepan over low heat, stirring until all the sugar has dissolved.

Careful! Make sure you can't see any more sugar crystals in the solution.

BLANCH THE APRICOTS

Put half the apricots in the pan to form a single layer in the syrup. Bring to a boil, and boil for 1 minute until the apricots are slightly soft but still hold their shape.

Remember Boiling the apricots in batches like this means that the water comes back to a boil quickly, and the fruits are covered and cook evenly.

Transfer the apricots to a sterilized jar with a slotted spoon and add half the almonds. Repeat with the rest of the batch.

ADD THE SYRUP AND AMARETTO

Put the pan back over the heat, bring the syrup to a boil, and pour it into the jar. Add enough amaretto to cover the apricots completely. Let cool. Seal and label the jar, then gently tip it upside down a couple of times to combine the syrup and alcohol. Store in a cool, dark place for 4 weeks for the flavors to mature, and refrigerate after opening.

Cherries in Brandy

3 small jars | **10 minutes, plus 4 weeks** | **12 months or longer**

Ingredients

1lb 2oz (500g) just-ripe sweet or Morello cherries, washed and de-stemmed

approx. ¾ cup granulated sugar

approx. 1½ cups brandy

FILL THE JARS WITH FRUIT

Discard any fruits that are not in perfect condition, then pack the rest into wide-necked sterilized preserving jars.

Help! If you are worried about how much fruit to pack into each jar, aim to add as many as you can without squishing or bruising them.

ADD SUGAR AND ALCOHOL

Add enough sugar to fill one-third of each jar. Pour in enough brandy to fill the jar completely and cover the fruit.

Tip Try to keep a ratio of ¼–⅓ sugar to ¾–⅔ alcohol when filling the jars to ensure that all the sugar dissolves in the alcohol and you don't end up with a gritty liqueur.

EXPEL AIR BUBBLES

Tap each jar gently on a work surface to release any air pockets and to ensure that no airborne microorganisms within the trapped air bubbles come into contact with the food and spoil it. Then seal, label, and store the jars in a cool, dark place.

DISSOLVE THE SUGAR AND MATURE

Occasionally turn the jars upside down over the next few days, or give them a shake to help the sugar dissolve in the alcohol. Store in a cool, dark place for 4 weeks to allow the flavors to mature, and refrigerate after opening.

Plums in Brandy variation Use the same quantities of plums, granulated sugar, and brandy. Prick the plums all over with a fork before canning them, and if the plums are large, halve and pit them instead.

Kumquats in Vodka

1 large jar

10 minutes, plus 2–3 months

12 months

Ingredients

1lb 2oz (500g) kumquats, washed, scrubbed, and dried

6 cardamom pods (optional)

approx. ¾ cup granulated sugar

approx. 1½ cups vodka

Special Equipment

cocktail stick or toothpick

FILL THE JARS WITH FRUIT

Prick the kumquats all over with a cocktail stick and pack into a sterilized preserving jar without squishing or bruising them.

Why? Pricking the fruit is vital as it allows the vodka syrup to penetrate the fruit, both preserving it and saturating it with flavor.

If you are using cardamom pods, crush them lightly with a pestle or the side of a knife. You want to split them without releasing the seeds.

ADD SUGAR AND ALCOHOL

Add enough sugar to fill one-third of the jar, then add enough vodka to completely cover the fruit.

Tip Try to keep a ratio of ¼–⅓ sugar to ¾–⅔ alcohol when filling the jar of fruit.

EXPEL AIR BUBBLES

Tap the jar gently on a work surface to release any air pockets, then seal and label. For the next few days, occasionally turn the jar upside down or give it a shake to help the sugar dissolve in the alcohol. Store in a cool, dark place for 2–3 months for the flavors to mature. Once opened, refrigerate and eat within 2 weeks.

Sloe Gin

1 large bottle | **20 minutes, plus 3 months** | **12 months**

Ingredients

approx. 8oz (225g) sloes, fresh or frozen (thawed to room temperature, if frozen)

⅓ cup granulated sugar

4 juniper berries, slightly crushed

a few drops of natural almond extract

approx. 1½ cups gin

Special Equipment

cocktail stick or toothpick

FILL THE JARS WITH FRUIT

Prick each sloe with a cocktail stick. If you are using frozen sloes, there is no need to prick them.

Why? Pricking the sloes releases more of their flavor. If you find this process too tiresome, simply freeze the sloes beforehand for a few hours instead—the freezing process softens the skins. If you are picking sloes after the first frosts, you similarly may not need to prick them.

Put the sloes in a sterilized bottle.

ADD SUGAR AND ALCOHOL

Add the sugar, juniper berries, and almond extract. Pour in enough gin to fill the bottle and cover the fruit. Seal and label the bottle.

Tip This recipe uses less sugar than some, so increase the quantities of sugar if you prefer a sweeter liqueur.

MIX THE INGREDIENTS

Shake the bottle gently or tip it upside down a few times to combine all the ingredients. Leave in a cool, dark place for 3 months, shaking the bottle occasionally.

STRAIN THE LIQUEUR

Strain the sloe gin into a sterilized bottle, seal, and use as required.

Plum Gin variation If you prefer (or if sloes aren't available), you can substitute plums for sloes. Keep all the quantities and all the other ingredients the same, but remember you may need a wider-necked bottle.

How to **Make Simple Salt Preserves**

Lemons and certain vegetables make delicious salted preserves; they develop a mellow, tangy flavor and softer texture. Most salted vegetables will last for several weeks or months if they are stored in the fridge; lemons should last for 6–9 months.

Use coarse sea salt to make the brine

Scrub waxed lemons with a vegetable brush to remove any wax

Salting in a colander

Some vegetables, such as cabbage, are preserved simply by drawing out their moisture with salt. Put the sliced vegetables in a large colander. Sprinkle salt over them and use your hands to toss the ingredients together; work in the salt thoroughly until the vegetable slices start to feel wet. Set the colander over a bowl and let stand at room temperature overnight. The bowl will catch the juice dripping from the vegetables.

Making a slow, cold brine

Tightly pack the fruit or vegetables into the jar. Add a generous amount of salt over each layer and into any gaps until you have used the amount recommended by the recipe. Fill the jar to the brim with boiled, cooled water, then seal it. Then, to encourage the salt to begin dissolving, gently shake the jar. Repeat this process every day for 2 weeks. The salt will gradually dissolve into the water to form brine.

Make sure the brine is boiling as you pour it into the jar, to keep it sterile

Pour in enough brine to fill the jar to the brim and cover the vegetables completely

Careful! Avoid using jars with unlined metal lids when canning: the lids will corrode and spoil the preserve. Always use jars with vinegar-proof lids, which have plasticized linings. For the best possible results, choose new lids, even if you recycle the jars.

Making a hot brine

This technique ensures the salt is dissolved from the start, by putting it in a saucepan with the water and heating gently, stirring until all the salt dissolves. Bring the brine to a boil and pour over a sterilized jar packed with the vegetables and any flavorings.

Preserved Lemons

1 large jar   **10 minutes,**   **6–9 months,**
           plus 3–4   **refrigerated**
           weeks

Ingredients

4 lemons, unwaxed

½ cup coarse sea salt

a few bay leaves

½ tsp black peppercorns

1 dried chile

a few cloves, or coriander or cumin
    seeds (optional)

freshly squeezed juice of 2 extra lemons

CUT THE LEMONS

Make a deep cut through each lemon from
the top, stopping two-thirds of the way down.
Then make a second deep cut at a right angle
to the first, so you end up with 4 lemon quarters
joined at the bottom.

PACK WITH SALT

Open out the cut quarters slightly and pack
salt into each crevice. Place the filled lemons in
a sterilized preserving jar and add the seasonings.
Add the remaining salt to the jar.

MAKE THE BRINE

Pour in the lemon juice and cover with cooled,
boiled water, if needed, to submerge the lemons and
fill the jar completely. Seal and store at room
temperature. Leave for 3–4 weeks for the lemon
rinds to soften. Shake or tip the jar upside down
occasionally to help the salt to dissolve and form
a brine. You can use the salted lemons in salads,
sauces, vinaigrettes, salsas, or tagines.

Salted Cucumbers with Dill

1 large jar **30 minutes, plus 4–6 weeks** **2 weeks, refrigerated once opened**

Ingredients

2 tbsp sea salt

4 tbsp dill, chopped

1 tbsp tarragon, chopped

1 tsp black peppercorns

1 tsp celery seeds

2 ridge cucumbers, about 7in (18cm) long, quartered lengthways, or approx. 8 small whole pickling cucumbers

4 pickling onions or shallots, peeled and thickly sliced

MAKE THE BRINE

Put the salt and 2 cups water into a saucepan and heat gently, stirring until the salt has dissolved and you can see no more salt crystals in the water. Bring to a boil and remove from the heat.

FILL THE JARS

Place half the fresh herbs, peppercorns, and celery seeds in the bottom of a sterilized preserving jar. Pack the cucumber quarters and sliced onions on top, and cover with the remaining herbs.

POUR IN THE BRINE

Add enough boiling brine to cover the cucumbers and flavorings completely. Seal, label, and store in a cool, dark place for 4–6 weeks. Once opened, store in the fridge.

Kimchi

1lb–1lb 5oz (450–600g) **25 minutes, plus 4–5 days** **2 weeks, refrigerated**

Ingredients

1 small head napa cabbage, cut into 2in (5cm) chunks

2 tbsp sea salt

4 scallions, chopped

1in (2.5cm) piece of fresh ginger, peeled and grated

1 garlic clove, crushed

¼ cup rice vinegar

1 tbsp Thai fish sauce (*nam pla*)

juice of 1 lime

2 tbsp sesame oil

2 tbsp toasted sesame seeds

2 tbsp sambal oelek

Special Equipment

large plastic container with a tight-fitting lid

SALT THE CABBAGE

Put the chopped cabbage into a colander set over a bowl. Add the salt and mix thoroughly with your hands until the cabbage is well coated.

Let stand overnight at room temperature. Next day, wash the leaves in water to remove all the salt. Drain and dry thoroughly on paper towels. Transfer to the plastic container, add the rest of the ingredients, and combine well. Seal.

MARINATE THE CABBAGE

Leave overnight to marinate at room temperature, then chill in the fridge for another few days. Keep refrigerated and use within 2 weeks.

How to **Make Pickles**

Pickling means to store produce in vinegar, which is a very effective preservative. A simple pickling process transforms fruit and vegetables into crisp, crunchy, versatile condiments with piquancy and bite. It's an easy two-stage process: salting or brining to draw out moisture, then submerging the produce in hot or cold vinegar.

Salting

To keep the pickled produce crisp, you need to remove its excess water. Put a layer of salt in a bowl and top with a layer of vegetable slices. Repeat the process, finishing with a good sprinkling of salt. Leave the bowl at room temperature for 24 hours, then wash off all the salt.

Dry salting is ideal for watery vegetables such as cucumbers, as it helps firm them up

Brining

Soaking in brine is best for less juicy produce. Dissolve salt in cold water to make a saline solution. Put the vegetables in a bowl and pour in enough solution to cover them completely. Leave in a cool place to soak for 12–48 hours, then rinse the vegetables. Removing some moisture from the vegetables also prevents the vinegar from becoming diluted, which would make it a less effective preservative.

Add roughly ¼ cup of salt for each 3½ cups of water

Soak vegetables in brine to extract their moisture and soften them slightly

Cold Pickling

Pack the vegetables into wide-necked sterilized jars. To make a crisp cold pickle, simply pour in enough cold vinegar to cover the vegetables completely, leaving a gap of ½ in (1cm) at the top of the jar. Seal the jars with non-metallic or vinegar-proof lids.

Add flavorings, such as garlic cloves, shallots, spices, and herbs, if you want

Pack the vegetables into the jars without overfilling them or pressing them down too tightly

Place dried herbs on a square of cheesecloth and tie with string

Make string long enough so it's easy to remove

Hot pickling

Use hot vinegar to give the pickled produce a softer texture, and add a spice bag for flavor. Boil the vinegar in a saucepan for about 5 minutes until it reduces by about a third, then carefully pour into the jars right up to the brim, so the vegetables are completely covered. Seal with non-metallic or vinegar-proof lids.

Pickled Gherkins

2 small jars	1 day, plus 3–4 weeks	6 months or longer

Ingredients

1lb 2oz (500g) small pickling cucumbers, washed well and rubbed with a cloth to dry and remove their fine down

½ cup sea salt

3–4 shallots, peeled and sliced

3–4 garlic cloves, peeled (optional)

2–3 dried chiles (optional)

½ tsp each coriander seeds, peppercorns, and dill seeds, or 1 crumbled dried bay leaf

2 sprigs dill, tarragon, or thyme

1 washed grape leaf (optional)

approx. 2½ cups white wine vinegar

PREPARE THE CUCUMBERS

Cut off any stalks and dried blossoms. Quarter the cucumbers lengthwise, or cut into ⅛in (3mm) slices, if they can't fit whole into the jars.

SALT THE CUCUMBERS

Put a little of the salt in a glass or ceramic bowl and add a layer of cucumbers. Cover the layer with more salt and repeat the process until all the cucumbers are arranged in the bowl. Sprinkle the last of the sea salt over the top. Leave for 24 hours at room temperature.

Remember By salting the cucumbers you are extracting some of their liquid and firming them up. This prevents excess water from being released into the jar and diluting the vinegar.

PACK INTO JARS

Wash the cucumbers to rinse off the salt and pack into sterilized jars, leaving ½in (1cm) at the top. Add the shallots, garlic cloves (if using), spices, and herbs. Use dill for a classic flavor and a grape leaf for crunch—the tannins in the leaves help keep the pickles crisp.

ADD THE VINEGAR

Pour in enough vinegar to cover the cucumbers completely. Seal with non-metallic or vinegar-proof lids, label, and store in a cool, dark place for 3–4 weeks, to mature.

Tip Remove the pickles with wooden tongs rather than a fork or spoon to prevent them from developing a metallic taste.

Mixed Vegetable Pickle

2 medium jars   **1 day, plus 10 days**   **3 months, refrigerated**

Ingredients

1 quart (1 liter) white wine vinegar

mixed whole spices (see method)

¼ cup sea salt

1 small cauliflower, chopped into florets

1 large onion, coarsely chopped

2 carrots, peeled and sliced

10 cherry tomatoes

5 jalapeño peppers, left whole (optional)

1 tsp coriander seeds

1 tsp mustard seeds

MAKE THE PICKLING VINEGAR

Place a selection of spices in a square of cheesecloth. You can use whatever whole spices you have on hand or all or any of the following: 1 tablespoon black peppercorns, ½ teaspoon cloves, 1 teaspoon crumbed mace blades, 1 tablespoon allspice berries, 1 tablespoon mustard seeds, 1 crushed dried red chile, 1 bay leaf, ½ crushed cinnamon stick, ½ tablespoon cardamom pods, and 2 crushed garlic cloves. Pour the vinegar into a pan, add the spice bag, and boil for 10 minutes. Set the pan aside and let cool before removing the spice bag. Pour the vinegar through a strainer into a glass bowl once cool.

SOAK IN BRINE

Make the brine by dissolving the salt in 2 cups of water in a large glass or ceramic bowl. Stir well to dissolve until no salt crystals are visible. Add the vegetables, cover with a plate to keep them submerged, and let stand overnight at room temperature.

Tip If the prepared vegetables together weigh more than 1lb 2oz (500g) and you need more brine, use a ratio of ⅓oz (10g) salt to ⅓ cup of water.

Mix the vinegar, coriander seeds, and mustard seeds in a jar and set aside.

PACK INTO JARS

Wash the vegetables in water to rinse off the salt, drain, and dry on paper towels. Layer in a sterilized jar and pour in the spiced vinegar mix to cover the vegetables completely. Seal with a non-metallic or vinegar-proof lid and label. Leave at room temperature for 2 days, then chill in the fridge for at least 1 week before opening. Once opened, keep refrigerated.

Red Cabbage Pickle

2 small jars   **1 day, plus 5–6 weeks**   **3 months, refrigerated**

Ingredients

1½lb (675g) red cabbage, cored and shredded

1 red onion, sliced

3 tbsp sea salt

2 cups white wine vinegar

½ cup light brown or granulated sugar

1 tsp mustard seeds

1 tsp coriander seeds

SALT THE CABBAGE

Mix the cabbage, onion, and salt in a large glass or ceramic bowl until the vegetables are coated in salt. Transfer to a colander set over a bowl and place a plate inside the colander to weigh down the ingredients. Leave overnight at room temperature.

Why? The salt removes the moisture from the cabbage leaves. The plate helps to bring more of the leaves' surface into contact with the salt.

MAKE THE VINEGAR MIX

Pour the vinegar into a large bowl, add the sugar and spices, and mix with a whisk to dissolve the sugar. Cover and leave overnight.

PREPARE THE VEGETABLES

Rinse the salt off the vegetables in cold running water. Drain and dry thoroughly with paper towels. The vegetables need to be completely dry to avoid diluting the vinegar.

PACK THE JARS

Pack the vegetables into sterilized jars. Stir the vinegar mix and pour it over the vegetables to completely cover them. Seal with non-metallic or vinegar-proof lids, label, and store in a cool, dark place for 1 week. Transfer to the fridge and store for 1 month for the flavors to mature. Once opened, keep refrigerated.

Careful! Make sure the vegetables are completely covered by the vinegar mix so that they are not exposed to airborne microbes.

Piccalilli

3 medium jars   **1 day, plus 1 month**   **6 months**

Ingredients

¼ cup sea salt

1 large cauliflower, cut into florets

2 large onions, peeled, quartered, and sliced finely, or use pickling onions

2lb (900g) mixed vegetables, such as zucchini, bell peppers, carrots, green beans, cut into bite-sized pieces

2 tbsp flour

1 cup granulated sugar

1 tbsp turmeric

¼ cup English mustard powder such as Colman's

900ml (1½ pints) spiced pickling vinegar (see p.59)

SOAK IN BRINE

Put the salt and 4 cups water in a large glass or ceramic bowl and mix well. Add the vegetables, cover with a plate to keep them submerged, and let stand overnight at room temperature.

BLANCH THE VEGETABLES

Wash the vegetables to rinse off the brine. Bring a large pan of water to a boil, add half of the vegetables, and blanch for about 2 minutes. Drain and immediately dip the vegetables in cold water to halt the cooking process. Repeat with the rest of the vegetables. It's important to keep the batches small, so as not to overcrowd the pan. The blanching process only begins when the water returns to a boil.

Tip Cook the vegetables until they are just *al dente* and still crunchy; don't overcook them.

MAKE THE SPICED VINEGAR SAUCE

Form a spice paste by putting the flour, sugar, turmeric powder, and mustard powder in a small bowl and mixing with a little vinegar. Transfer to a large stainless-steel saucepan, pour in the rest of the vinegar, and bring to a boil, stirring constantly.

Why? Mixing the ingredients into a paste binds them together. As you add the vinegar it dilutes the ingredients to a loose paste and then a smooth sauce. Stirring the sauce continuously ensures the ingredients won't separate and form lumps.

Simmer the spiced vinegar for 15 minutes, then remove from the heat. Add the vegetables, stir until well coated in the sauce, ladle into warm, sterilized mason jars, leaving ¼in (5mm) headspace, and ensure there are no air gaps. Cover, seal with a two-part top, then heat process for 10 minutes (see pp.116–121). Label and store in a cool, dark place for at least 1 month. Once opened, keep refrigerated.

Tip Press the piccalilli down as you fill the jars to remove any air pockets. This will ensure that no airborne microbes in the trapped air bubbles come into contact with the food and spoil it.

How to **Make Freezer Pickles**

Freezer pickles don't need the same quantities of vinegar, salt, and sugar as traditional pickles to preserve them; the freezing process acts as an effective preservative. It also helps to retain the vegetables' color, flavor, and crunch. The vinegar, salt, and sugar are added to the familiar taste of a pickle.

Press the vegetable slices down to extract more moisture

Salting

Sprinkle salt over the vegetable slices and leave for 2 hours to extract their moisture. This helps retain their texture when frozen and once thawed. Rinse off the salt to avoid making the slices too salty, drain well, and pat dry to remove the last of the moisture.

Pickling

Pour a solution of vinegar, sugar, and spices over the vegetables and refrigerate overnight so the flavors can mature. There's no need to completely cover the vegetables; freezing will provide the sterile, airless environment traditionally provided by the vinegar.

The vinegar solution acts like a marinade or acidifier rather than a sealant that excludes air

Bread and Butter Freezer Pickle

12oz–1lb (350–450g)   **2¼ hours**   **6 months**

Ingredients

2 large cucumbers, scrubbed and sliced thinly

2 shallots, very finely sliced

½ green bell pepper, finely chopped (optional)

1–2 tsp sea salt

½ cup cider or wine vinegar

⅛–¼ cup granulated sugar

a good pinch of ground turmeric

a good pinch of celery or dill seeds,
    or ½–1 tsp mustard seeds

SALT THE VEGETABLES

Mix the cucumbers, shallots, pepper (if using), and salt in a large glass or ceramic bowl until the vegetables are completely coated in salt. Leave for 2 hours at room temperature.

Remember The salt will draw moisture from the vegetables.

PREPARE THE VEGETABLES

Transfer the vegetables to a colander and wash to rinse off the salt. Drain well, pressing them down lightly with your hand to extract the moisture. Transfer to a dry bowl.

MARINATE IN THE SPICED VINEGAR

Mix the vinegar and sugar to taste, stirring to dissolve the sugar. Add the spices and pour the spiced vinegar over the vegetables. Cover with a plate and marinate overnight in the fridge to develop a classic pickle flavor before being frozen.

Why? It's important to marinate before freezing because the flavors won't deepen and mingle once the pickle is frozen.

Tip If you like a sharp pickle, add less salt. For a milder pickle add more sugar.

PLACE IN CONTAINERS

Divide the pickle between portion-sized freezer containers, leaving ½in (1cm) of space at the top to allow for expansion. Seal, label, date, and freeze. To use, thaw it in the fridge overnight first, then keep it refrigerated and consume within 1 week.

How to **Make Chutney**

Chutneys are versatile sweet-sour mixtures of vegetables, fruits, spices, and dried fruits, which are cooked slowly in vinegar, salt, and sugar to preserve them effectively. The heat produced as the chutney cooks also helps kill most microbes. There are only a couple of simple guidelines to follow to make this tasty savory preserve with a bite!

Chop the fruits and vegetables into small pieces to give the chutney a good texture

Use a stainless-steel saucepan and a wooden spoon, as these won't react with the vinegar

Cook the mixture slowly

Slow-cooking is the golden rule. Stir the chopped fruit, vegetables, spices, sugar, and vinegar mixture occasionally as it cooks. But as it thickens, stir more frequently so it doesn't stick to the bottom of the pan and burn, which would give the chutney a burnt, bitter flavor.

Tip Sugar is a vital ingredient in any chutney, as it prevents the flesh and skins of fruits and vegetables softening too much and turning mushy. It's important to dissolve the sugar before you bring the mixture to a boil.

Reduce until the liquid has evaporated and the sugar and vinegar are at the optimum concentrations for preserving

The colors of the ingredients darken and the flavors intensify as the chutney cooks

Testing

Draw a wooden spoon across the bottom of the pan. If it leaves a clear trail for a few seconds, the chutney is ready. If lots of liquid covers the trail immediately, cook the chutney a little longer and keep testing it. Once canned, let it mature for at least 1 month before consuming.

Practice MAKING CHUTNEY

Plum Chutney

The secret of deliciously tangy chutney is time: a long,
gentle cooking time, and then time for it to mature before
being opened. This basic recipe is ideal for all kinds of
seasonal produce, so experiment with different fruits and
vegetables—just keep the overall quantities the same.

3 large jars — Approx. 2 hours, plus 1–2 months — 12 months

plums

apples

onions

Ingredients

2¼lb (1kg) plums

12oz (350g) apples

9oz (250g) onions

4½oz (125g) raisins

1½ cups light brown sugar

1 tsp sea salt

1 tsp each allspice, cinnamon, and coriander, freshly ground if possible

1 chile or ½ tsp dried chile flakes

1 tsp fennel seeds (optional)

2 cups white wine or cider vinegar

raisins

light brown sugar

sea salt

spices

dried chile flakes

fennel seeds

white wine vinegar

sharp knife

cutting board

Equipment

sharp chopping knife

cutting board

stainless steel preserving pan or large, heavy-bottomed stainless steel saucepan

large wooden spoon

wide-mouthed jam funnel

ladle

jars with vinegar-proof lids, or with cellophane covers and elastic bands

discs of waxed paper

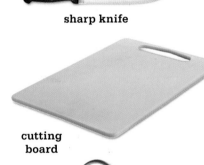
preserving pan

wooden spoon

wide-mouthed jam funnel

ladle

jars

discs of waxed paper and cellophane covers

1 Peel and finely slice the onions. Halve the plums, remove their pits, and cut the fruit into quarters. Core, peel, and coarsely dice the apples into bite-sized pieces.

Tip You can use slightly overripe or slightly imperfect produce, but carefully cut out and discard any bruised or damaged parts. The quality of the chutney depends on this kind of meticulous approach.

Chop the ingredients into small, evenly sized pieces so the chutney will have a good texture and a spoonable consistency

Use a wooden spoon to stir the mixture until the sugar has dissolved

2 Put all the ingredients into a preserving pan or a large heavy-bottomed, stainless steel saucepan and bring slowly to a boil, stirring to dissolve the sugar.

Why? It's important to use a stainless steel pan and not a brass, copper, or iron pan, as these metals will react with the vinegar and give the finished chutney a metallic taste.

3 Turn the heat down and simmer gently for 1–1½ hours. Test the chutney by dragging a wooden spoon through the mixture along the bottom of the pan.

Careful! Make sure you stir the chutney frequently toward the end of the cooking time, so it doesn't catch and burn on the bottom of the pan.

The chutney is ready if a clear channel remains. It should have a thick, jam-like consistency and look glossy

Use a funnel to fill the sterilized jars with chutney

Stand the jars on a tray or board to catch any drips

Make sure there are no air pockets in the filled jars

4 Check the seasoning and ladle into warm, sterilized jars, leaving ¼in (5mm) headspace. Cover, seal with a two-part top, heat process for 5 minutes (pp.116–121), then label.

Careful! Vinegar corrodes metal, so use plastic lids or metal lids that have a plastic seal or cover.

How to store

Store the sealed jars in a cool, dark place and leave to mature for 1–2 months. Chutneys can taste harsh and flat if eaten immediately.

Did anything go wrong?

The chutney has shrunk inside the jar. It has lost moisture, probably because the lid wasn't airtight. Make sure you seal each jar carefully.

Liquid has collected at the top of the jar. The chutney wasn't cooked for long enough. Cook it gently until the liquid evaporates.

The chutney has started to ferment. The vinegar solution was too weak, the storage conditions are too warm, or the chutney wasn't cooked long enough. Discard the chutney.

There is mold or an unpleasant odor. The chutney may have been contaminated; discard the chutney and sterilize all your equipment.

Try more Chutney recipes ▶ ▶ ▶

Green Bean and Zucchini Chutney

3 medium jars   **2 hours**   **9 months**

Ingredients

1lb 5oz (600g) large green beans, thinly sliced

4 zucchini, thinly sliced

12oz (350g) apples, peeled, cored, and chopped

2 onions, finely chopped

2¼ cups light brown sugar

1 tsp mustard powder

1 tsp turmeric

1 tsp coriander seeds

2 cups cider vinegar

COOK THE INGREDIENTS

Put all the ingredients in a preserving pan or large, heavy-bottomed stainless-steel saucepan. Cook over low heat, stirring until the sugar has dissolved. Bring to a boil and cook at a rolling boil for 10 minutes, stirring occasionally. Then reduce the heat and simmer the mixture gently for about 1½ hours.

Careful! Stir continuously toward the end of the cooking time to prevent the mixture from sticking and burning on the bottom of the pan.

LADLE INTO JARS

Test whether the chutney is ready by drawing a spoon across the bottom of the pan to see if it leaves a clear trail. Ladle into warm, sterilized mason jars, leaving ¼in (5mm) headspace, and

ensure there are no air gaps. Cover and seal with a two-part top, then heat process for 10 minutes (see pp.116–121). Label and store in a cool, dark place for at least 1 month for the flavors to mature and mellow. Once opened, keep refrigerated.

Tip Press the chutney down as you fill the jars to remove any air pockets where microbes can grow.

Tomato and Roasted Pepper Chutney

3 medium jars **2 hours 20 minutes** **9 months**

Ingredients

1 red bell pepper

1 orange bell pepper

1 yellow bell pepper

3lb (1.35kg) ripe tomatoes

2 onions, coarsely chopped

2 cups granulated sugar

2 cups white wine vinegar

PREPARE THE PEPPERS

Preheat the oven to 400°F (200°C). Arrange the peppers on a baking sheet and roast for 25–30 minutes until they are slightly charred. Meanwhile, prepare the tomatoes by plunging them into boiling water for 1 minute and then peeling. When the peppers are cooked and still hot, put them in a plastic bag and let cool. Once cool, take the peppers out of the plastic bag and simply pull off the skins with your fingers and discard. Seed, remove the stems, and chop the flesh coarsely.

Why? Cooling the peppers in a plastic bag creates condensation and makes them easy to peel.

CHOP THE VEGETABLES

Put the peeled tomatoes, chopped peppers, and onions in a food processor and pulse briefly until chopped but not mushy. Alternatively, chop the vegetables by hand.

COOK THE INGREDIENTS

Put all the ingredients in a preserving pan or large, heavy-bottomed stainless-steel saucepan. Cook over low heat, stirring until the sugar has dissolved. Bring to a boil, then reduce the heat and

simmer the mixture gently for about 1½ hours, until it thickens to a jam-like texture.

Careful! Stir continuously toward the end so the mixture does not catch on the bottom of the pan and burn.

LADLE INTO JARS

Test whether the chutney is ready by drawing a spoon across the bottom of the pan to see if it leaves a clear trail. Ladle into warm, sterilized mason jars, leaving ¼in (5mm) headspace, and ensure there are no air gaps. Cover and seal with a two-part top, then heat process for 10 minutes (see pp.116–121). Label and store in a cool, dark place, allowing the flavors to mature for at least 1 month. Once opened, keep refrigerated.

How to **Make Relish**

Part pickle, part chutney, relishes are crunchy, sweet-sour condiments of diced fruit and vegetables, sugar, and vinegar—often with a hint of spice. Relishes enhance any dish and are even easier to make than chutneys, as they are cooked for less time and are less concentrated—although this also means that they don't keep for as long.

To test, draw a spoon across the bottom of the pan to see that very little liquid is left

Relish should be of a spoonable consistency

Make small quantities of relish as it doesn't last as long as chutney

Cook gently

Dice the vegetables for a fine, spoonable texture. Put the ingredients in a large pan. Stir over low heat to dissolve the sugar and bring to a boil. Let it simmer for 15–20 minutes, stirring frequently, until it is slightly thick and most of the liquid has evaporated.

Canning

When the relish is still quite wet, remove it from the heat and can into warm sterilized jars using a ladle. Seal the jars with non-metallic or vinegar-proof lids. Relish can be eaten immediately, but must be stored in the fridge once opened.

Sweet Corn and Pepper Relish

2 small
jars

35–40
minutes

3 months

Ingredients

4 cobs sweet corn

2 medium red bell peppers, or 1 green and
    1 red bell pepper, seeded and finely diced

2 celery stalks, finely sliced

1 red chile, seeded and finely sliced (optional)

1 medium onion, finely sliced

2 cups white wine vinegar

1 cup granulated sugar

2 tsp sea salt

2 tsp mustard powder

½ tsp ground turmeric

PREPARE THE SWEET CORN

Separate the kernels from the cobs by holding
a cob upright in one hand and running a sharp knife
down the sides to slice off the kernels. Bring a pan of
water to a boil and blanch the corn kernels in the
boiling water for 2 minutes. Drain well.

COOK THE INGREDIENTS

Put all the ingredients into a preserving pan or
large, heavy-bottomed stainless-steel saucepan
and heat the mixture, stirring to dissolve the sugar.
Bring to a boil, turn the heat down, and simmer
gently, stirring often, for 15–20 minutes.

CAN THE RELISH

Test whether the relish is ready by drawing
a spoon across the bottom of the pan. If just a little
liquid is left, the relish is ready. Ladle into warm,
sterilized mason jars, leaving ½in (1cm) headspace.
Cover, seal with a two-part top, then heat process
for 10 minutes (see pp.116–121), and label. Once
opened, keep refrigerated.

Tip The relish goes well with burgers and
barbecued meats and can be consumed
immediately, although the flavors will improve
after a few weeks in storage.

Spicy Carrot Relish

1 small jar | Approx. 1 hour | 3 months

Ingredients

2 tsp coriander seeds

handful of cardamom pods

1in (2.5cm) piece of fresh ginger

1lb 2oz (500g) carrots, grated

1 tsp mustard seeds

juice and zest of 1 orange

½ cup cider vinegar

½ cup granulated or light brown sugar

PREPARE THE SPICES

Crush the coriander seeds lightly in a mortar and pestle. Extract the cardamom seeds from the pod by lightly crushing with a pestle and then pulling the skin apart with your fingers. You need about 1 teaspoon of seeds. Peel the ginger using the edge of a teaspoon, then finely grate it.

COOK THE INGREDIENTS

Put the carrots and mustard, coriander, and cardamom seeds into a preserving pan or large, heavy-bottomed saucepan and stir. Add the ginger, orange juice and zest, vinegar, and sugar and heat the mixture, stirring until the sugar dissolves. Cook gently for 10 minutes, stirring often, to soften the carrots. Turn up the heat a little and let the mixture simmer, stirring frequently, for 15–20 minutes.

CAN THE RELISH

Test if the relish is ready by drawing a spoon across the pan's bottom to see if just a little liquid is left. Ladle into a clean, hot, sterilized mason jar with ½in (1cm) headspace. Cover with a waxed paper disc, seal with vinegar-proof lids and rings, and heat process for 10 minutes (see pp.116–121). Label and store in a cool, dark place for at least 1 month. Once opened, keep refrigerated. Goes well with curry.

Tomato Relish

1 medium jar | 1 hour 40 minutes | 6 months

Ingredients

2¼lb (1kg) ripe tomatoes, peeled if you prefer

2 onions, coarsely chopped

3 zucchini, coarsely chopped

1 yellow bell pepper, seeded and coarsely chopped

2 garlic cloves

2 red chiles or jalapeño chiles, stems removed (or more if you like it hot)

2 tbsp tomato paste

1 tsp English mustard powder, such as Coleman's

1¼ cups malt or cider vinegar

⅔ cup granulated sugar

CHOP THE VEGETABLES

Either chop the tomatoes, onions, zucchini, pepper, garlic, and chile by hand or process in separate batches in a food processor. Pulse until chopped, but not chopped too fine.

COOK THE INGREDIENTS

Put the chopped vegetables in a preserving pan or a large, heavy-bottomed stainless-steel saucepan. Stir in the tomato paste and mustard powder, then add the vinegar and sugar. Simmer, stirring continously, until the sugar has dissolved, then turn the heat up and cook steadily for 40 minutes–1 hour, stirring frequently, or until the mixture begins to thicken.

CAN THE RELISH

Ladle into a clean, hot, sterilized mason jar with ½in (1cm) headspace. Seal with a non-metallic or vinegar-proof lid and ring, then heat process for 10 minutes (see pp.116–121). Label and store in a cool, dark place for at least 1 month for the flavors to mature. Once opened, keep refrigerated.

Beet Relish

2 small jars **2¼ hours** **9 months**

Ingredients

3lb (1.35kg) raw beets

1 tsp granulated sugar

1lb (450g) shallots, finely chopped

2 cups cider or white wine vinegar

1 tbsp pickling spices, sealed in cheesecloth
(see p.57)

Special Equipment

small square of cheesecloth and string

COOK THE BEETS

Put the beets and sugar in a preserving pan or large, heavy-bottomed stainless-steel saucepan, cover with water, and bring to a boil. Simmer for 1 hour or until the beets are soft and cooked. Drain and set aside to cool. Once cold, peel and dice.

Careful! Beets can stain skin and clothes. If you don't want your fingers to get stained, peel the beets wearing clean rubber gloves.

COOK THE RELISH

Rinse out the pan, add the shallots and vinegar, and cook over low heat for 10 minutes. Add the diced beets and the bag of pickling spices, stir the mixture, and add the sugar. Stir until the sugar has dissolved and bring to a boil. Cook at a rolling boil for 5 minutes, then reduce the heat and simmer the relish for 40 minutes or until it thickens.

CAN THE RELISH

Draw a spoon across the bottom of the pan to see if the relish is ready—there should be only a little liquid left. Remove the spice bag and ladle into clean, hot, sterilized mason jars with ½in (1cm) headspace. Cover with waxed paper discs, seal with non-metallic or vinegar-proof lids and rings, and heat process for 10 minutes (see pp.116–121). Once opened, keep refrigerated.

Tip This relish is best stored in a cool, dark place for 1 month to allow the flavors to mature fully, although it can be eaten immediately. It goes well with cheeses or beef.

2
Build On It

This chapter expands your knowledge of, and confidence in, preserving. It will allow you to really get comfortable with some of the classic techniques for preserving fruit—such as jams and jellies—that tend to involve a little more skill than savory preserves.

In this section, learn to prepare or make:

Fruit Cheese
pp.78–85

Jam
pp.86–97

Conserve
pp.98–101

Jelly
pp.102–109

Syrups and Cordials
pp.110–115

Fruits in Syrup
pp.116–123

Dried Fruit and Vegetables
pp.124–131

How to **Make Fruit Cheese**

Fruit cheese is a misleading name, as this preserve doesn't actually contain any dairy—or taste much like it—although it does go well with cheese! Fruit cheeses are intensely flavored fruit purées that have been cooked with sugar until they are concentrated, and are solid enough to slice once they cool. The related fruit butters are less intense, lightly sweetened purées with a spreadable texture.

Cook the fruit until it is soft and pulpy

Use a measuring cup to calculate how much purée you have

Cook and strain the fruit

Simmer chopped fruit with some water in a preserving pan or large saucepan until it turns to a pulp. Then pass the fruit pulp—in batches, if necessary—through a strainer or foodmill. Set the strainer over a large, clean bowl to collect the purée.

Measure the purée

Next, measure the purée so you know how much sugar has to be added. Spoon the purée into a measuring cup. You need 2 cups of granulated sugar for every 2 cups of cooked, strained fruit pulp that you measure.

> **Tip** To make fruit butter, simply stop the cooking halfway through the slow-cooking process. At this point, the purée should be a thick, but not yet stiff, paste. It's ready when a spoon pressed down on it leaves a clear indent.

The sugar has dissolved when you can't feel any grittiness on the bottom of the pan

The paste should ooze slowly as you spoon or pour it into a mold

Reduce to paste

Put the purée in a clean pan and add the sugar. Cook over low heat, stirring with a wooden spoon until the sugar dissolves. Bring to a boil, then turn the heat down and slow cook for the required amount of time, stirring occasionally.

Pour into molds

The fruit cheese is ready when it looks dark, thick, and glossy, sticks to the spoon, and leaves a trail if you draw the spoon across the bottom of the pan. When ready, pour the fruit cheese into greased sterilized molds and leave to cool and set.

Membrillo

A traditional Spanish delicacy, often served with Manchego cheese, this lightly scented fruit cheese is made from quince, which are cooked down into a thick, stiff paste. It has a concentrated flavor and keeps for a long time. Always use delicious fruit in prime condition for this versatile preserve.

6 ramekin dishes **1½ hours** **12 months or longer**

Ingredients

2¼lb (1kg) quince, scrubbed and chopped

juice of ½ lemon

approx. 2 cups granulated sugar

peanut or sunflower oil, for greasing

quince

lemon juice

granulated sugar

Equipment

preserving pan or large, heavy-bottomed saucepan

large wooden spoon

fine mesh strainer

large, clean bowl

measuring cup

ramekins or other ceramic molds, or a shallow baking dish

parchment paper and string (optional)

preserving pan

wooden spoon

strainer

bowl

measuring cup

ramekin

1 Put the chopped quinces in a preserving pan or a large heavy-bottomed saucepan with 2 cups of water and the lemon juice. Bring to a boil and simmer for 30 minutes, and when the fruit is soft, lightly crush with a potato masher or fork.

Remember There is no need to peel or core the quinces before you chop them, as you will be straining the cooked fruit.

Scrape down the underside of the strainer after each batch, before discarding the waste pulp

2 Remove the pan from the heat and let cool slightly. Then strain the pulp in batches over a large, clean bowl. Measure the purée: for every 2 cups of purée, add 2 cups of sugar.

Tip Press the pulp hard against the side of the fine mesh strainer with a wooden spoon to extract as much of the purée as possible.

3 Put the purée back in the pan, add the sugar, and stir over low heat to dissolve the sugar. Bring to a boil, then simmer gently for 45–60 minutes, stirring only occasionally at first.

Careful! Start stirring the purée more regularly toward the end of the cooking time, so it does not catch and burn on the bottom of the pan.

The mix will bubble and spit, so be careful

4 Test the paste to see if it is ready by dragging a wooden spoon across the bottom of the pan. The paste should leave a trail, look stiff and glossy, and stick to the spoon when it is ready.

Tip For extra taste, you can add unusual flavorings, such as rosewater or aromatic liqueurs, near the end of the cooking time, before you pour the paste into molds.

Stir the mixture often, especially near the end of the cooking time

The fruit cheese will turn solid as it cools

5 Lightly grease warm, sterilized ramekin dishes or molds with a little oil. Spoon in the paste, level the top, and let cool. To store, seal the molds with waxed paper discs and cellophane.

Tip If you want to reuse the ramekins once the membrillo has cooled, loosen the molds with a palette knife, turn out the membrillo, and wrap each in parchment and tie with string.

How to store

Membrillo can be stored for 12 months or longer. When you need it, turn it out of the mold (or unwrap it) and slice it finely.

Store all fruit cheeses in a cool, dark place for at least 4–6 weeks to mature in flavor.

Try other fruit

Other good fruits for fruit cheeses and butters include plums, pears, apples (combined with quinces or plums for a fruit cheese), boysenberries, grapes, loganberries, winter squash, mulberries, and pumpkin.

Try more Fruit Cheese recipes ▶ ▶ ▶

Damson Cheese

3 ramekin dishes **2–2½ hours** **2 years**

Ingredients

2¼lb (1kg) damson plums, pitted and chopped

granulated sugar (see method)

1–2 tbsp butter (optional)

MAKE A PURÉE

Simmer the fruit in a preserving pan or large, heavy-bottomed saucepan with 1¼ cups water for 30–40 minutes until it is a thick pulp. Crush the fruit with the back of a fork or potato masher as it cooks. Pour the pulp into a fine strainer held over a bowl and collect the juice and purée.

Pour the purée into a measuring cup and add the sugar. For every 2 cups of purée, add 2 cups of sugar. Taste the purée and if it seems a little sharp, mix in an additional 5¼oz (150g) of sugar per 1 pint (600ml) of purée. Put the purée, sugar, and butter, if using, back in the pan, stir over low heat to dissolve the sugar, and slowly bring to a boil.

Tip Adding butter helps to soften and mellow the sharp flavor of the damsons.

COOK GENTLY

Simmer the purée gently for 35–45 minutes, or longer, stirring often, until it forms a glossy paste and "plops."

Careful! Stir regularly to ensure the purée doesn't catch and burn on the bottom of the pan.

Test whether the cheese is ready by drawing a spoon across the bottom of the pan to see if it leaves a clear trail.

FILL AND STORE

Oil 3 ramekin dishes lightly and fill with the cheese. Cover with waxed paper discs and plastic wrap and let cool. Turn out of ramekins and wrap in waxed paper or plastic wrap. Label and store in a cool, dark place for at least 6–8 weeks to mature. Damson cheese works well sliced with cold meats and cheeses or as an after-dinner treat.

Apple Butter

3 medium jars   **2 hours 25 minutes**   **6 months**

Ingredients

2lb (900g) apples, coarsely chopped

juice of 1 orange

pinch of ground allspice

pinch of ground cinnamon

3 cups granulated sugar

MAKE A PURÉE

Simmer the apples in a preserving pan or large heavy-bottomed saucepan with 1 cup water for 10 minutes until they are soft. Pour the fruit pulp into a fine strainer held over a bowl and collect the juice and purée.

COOK GENTLY

Put the purée back in the pan and add the orange juice, ground allspice, cinnamon, and sugar. Stir over low heat to dissolve the sugar and slowly bring to a boil. Simmer the purée gently for 2 hours or longer, stirring every so often so that it doesn't catch and burn on the bottom of the pan, until it thickens.

TEST THE BUTTER

The butter is ready when a spoon drawn across the bottom of the pan leaves a clear trail. The butter should also be thick enough to rest on the back of the spoon without running off.

CAN IN JARS

Ladle into warm, sterilized mason jars, leaving ¼in (5mm) headspace. Cover, seal with a two-part top, then heat process for 5-10 minutes (pp.116–121). Label and store in a cool, dark place. Once opened, keep refrigerated. Apple butter keeps for up to 6 months and goes well with good, fresh bread and in desserts.

How to **Make Jam**

Jam-making is a popular pursuit, and a skill that's immensely satisfying to learn. The concept is simple: fruit is preserved with sugar by cooking over high heat until it sets. As the fruit cooks it releases the gum-like substance called pectin, which is a natural setting agent. For a good set, the balance of sugar, pectin, and acid must be correct (see pp.88–89).

Soften the fruit and add sugar

The fruit is prepared according to the recipe and simmered in water until soft. Pour the sugar into the pan and stir with a wooden spoon until the sugar has completely dissolved.

Careful! Do not add the sugar until the fruit has cooked enough to become soft and release its pectin: sugar inhibits the release of pectin and toughens the fruit skins.

Dissolve the sugar over low heat so the jam does not become grainy

Boil rapidly

Turn the heat up high and bring the mixture to a rapid, rolling boil to give the pectin time to set with the sugar. Rapidly boiling jam rises in the pan and becomes frothy with masses of small bubbles; it should – theoretically—set when the sugar reaches 220°F (105°C). If you don't have a sugar thermometer, start testing for set when the bubbles become larger and start to "plop."

The jam should have reached setting point when it reaches 220°F (105°C)

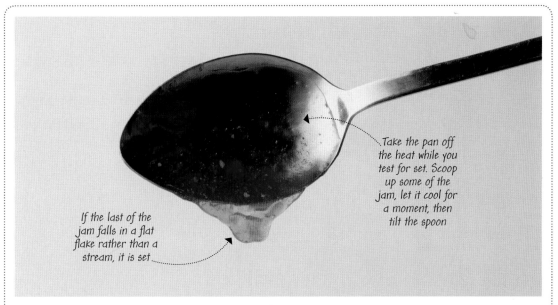

Take the pan off the heat while you test for set. Scoop up some of the jam, let it cool for a moment, then tilt the spoon

If the last of the jam falls in a flat flake rather than a stream, it is set

Flake test

Take the pan off the heat and put 1 teaspoon jam on the cold saucer. Let it cool, then push it to one side with your finger. If it wrinkles and your finger leaves a trail, it is set

To get rapid results when testing, place some saucers in the fridge to chill while you make the jam

Wrinkle test

Test for a set

Jam sets when it has been sufficiently cooked, typically between 5 and 20 minutes. Take the pan off the heat and test for set sooner rather than later: over-done jam is hard, rubbery, and difficult to salvage, but if jam is runny and not quite ready, continue boiling and test it again.

Understanding **Pectin and Acid in Fruit**

Jam forms when pectin—the gum-like substance released as the fruit simmers —reacts with sugar and acid to make a jelly. The natural acid found in fruit helps to release the pectin and avoid a lengthy cooking process (which might spoil the taste of the jam) while the sugar enables the pectin to gel. The crucial factor in achieving a jelly, or "set," is to have the right balance of pectin and acid.

*Sharp or tart tasting fruits, such as **crab apples**, tend to have higher acid content*

*Low-pectin fruits, such as **pears**, need extra pectin and acid to achieve a set.*

*High-pectin fruits, such as **red currants**, set easily to give a solid set, and absorb more sugar.*

*Medium-pectin fruits, such as **apricots**, set satisfactorily, usually giving a softer set.*

Adding extra acid

If the acid levels of a particular fruit are low (see table), add extra acid when you begin the cooking process to help the fruit release its pectin and achieve a set. The acid also helps to improve the color and flavor of jam and prevent sugar crystallization. There are two ways to increase the acid levels:

Add lemon juice. Add the juice of 1 lemon (2 tablespoons) for every 2¹/₄lb (1kg) fruit you use.

Add citric or tartaric acid, available from pharmacies. For every 2¹/₄lb (1kg) fruit you use, add ¹/₂ teaspoon citric or tartaric acid dissolved in 4 tablespoons water.

Jam sugar

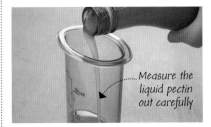

Measure the liquid pectin out carefully

Liquid pectin

Powdered pectin

Adding extra pectin

There are several options for fruits that lack enough natural pectin to make a set, however if you need to add a lot of pectin you may have to adjust the amount of sugar in the recipe to compensate. Jam sugar is specially formulated to contain the correct balance of pectin and sugar. Powdered and liquid pectin is commercially available; mix powdered pectin into the sugar before you add to the fruit. Liquid pectin is very concentrated; follow the manufacturer's instructions.

Pectin and Acid Content of Key Fruits

For the best results choose slightly under-ripe fruit for jam-making because pectin levels tend to decrease as fruit ages. The riper the fruit, the less pectin it's likely to contain.

Fruits	Pectin Content	Acidity
Black currants	High	High
Crab apples	High	High
Cranberries (unripe)	High	Medium
Gooseberries	High	High
Plums (unripe), damsons	High	High
Quinces	High	High–medium
Red and white currants	High	High
Citrus fruits (pectin is found in the skins, peel, and pith)	High–medium	High–medium
Cooking apples	High–medium	High–medium
Apricots	Medium	Medium
Cranberries (ripe)	Medium	Medium
Grapes (unripe) (variable pectin content)	Medium	Medium
Loganberries	Medium	Medium
Medlars	Medium	Low
Morello (cooking) cherries	Medium	Medium
All plums (ripe)	Medium	Medium
Raspberries	Medium	Medium
Blackberries	Low–medium	Low
Blueberries (variable pectin content)	Low–medium	Low
Wild blackberries (brambles)	Low	Low
Cherries (dessert)	Low	Low
Figs	Low	Low
Grapes (ripe) (variable pectin content)	Low	Low
Melons	Low	Low
Nectarines	Low	Low
Peaches	Low	Low
Pears	Low	Low
Rhubarb	Low	High
Strawberries	Low	Low

Raspberry Jam

Homemade jam has a delicious depth of flavor
and fruity freshness that you don't find in store-bought
produce. This straightforward recipe produces a lovely
soft-set raspberry jam, and is also suitable to
use with other soft-skinned berries.

2 small jars   **25–30 minutes**   **6 months**

raspberries   **lemon juice**   **granulated sugar**

Ingredients

1½lb (650g) raspberries
  (preferably not overripe)

juice of ½ lemon

2¼ cups granulated sugar

Equipment

preserving pan or large,
  heavy-bottomed saucepan

large wooden spoon

sugar thermometer (optional)

sterilized wide-mouthed jam
  funnel (optional)

ladle

skimmer or slotted spoon (optional)

sterilized jars with metal lids or
  cellophane covers and elastic bands

discs of waxed paper

preserving pan   **wooden spoon**

**sugar
thermometer**

**wide-mouthed
jam funnel**

ladle

slotted spoon

jars

elastic bands

**discs of waxed paper
and cellophane covers**

1 Put a few small saucers in the fridge to chill. Place the fruit in a preserving pan or large, heavy-bottomed saucepan. Add the lemon juice and ⅔ cup of water. The lemon juice provides extra acid, which is vital for setting, as raspberries tend to be low in acid.

Tip Ensure the berries are in perfect condition and use soon after picking. Wash them only if they need it, as dry fruit is best.

Raspberries that aren't overripe are best for making jam

Keep the heat low until the sugar has completely dissolved

2 Simmer the fruit gently for 3–5 minutes to soften and release its juices. Then add the sugar and stir it in over low heat. Once it has all dissolved, turn the heat to high.

Remember Sugar inhibits the release of pectin and toughens the skins of fruits, so always add it to the pan after the fruit has softened sufficiently.

3 Bring the jam to a rolling boil for 5–10 minutes or until the setting point is reached. Start testing for the setting point when the bubbles in the jam become large and start "plopping."

Help! If you are worried about missing the setting point, it is better to test early and frequently than wait too long before testing.

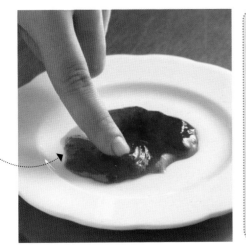

Push the jam to one side with your finger to see if it wrinkles slightly

4 Take the pan off the heat to test for a set. If you are doing a wrinkle test (see p.87), use one of the cold saucers placed in the fridge earlier.

Tip If you want to double-check the jam is set, use a flake test: put a little jam in a bowl, scoop some up with a spoon, let it cool for a moment, and tilt the spoon. If the last of the jam falls in a flat flake rather than a stream, it is set.

5 Ladle into clean, hot, sterilized mason jars with ¼in (5mm) headspace using a sterilized jam funnel. Cover with waxed paper discs, seal with lids and rings, and heat process for 5 minutes (see pp.116–121).

Help! If there is foam on the surface of the jam, use a skimmer to remove it before you can, or stir the jam in the same direction until the foam has dispersed.

Jam funnels have wide mouths and brims to catch any drips

How to store

Label and store your batches of jam in a cool, dark place. They will keep for about 6–9 months. Refrigerate after opening; use within 3–4 weeks.

Did anything go wrong?

Jam that won't set is under-boiled or too low in pectin. Try boiling it again briefly with commercial pectin. If it still doesn't set, re-boil with lemon juice.

If your jam is flavorless, dull, and hard, it is over-boiled. Start testing sooner next time, and always turn off the heat while you test for a set.

If your jam ferments, you may have over-boiled it, used overripe fruit, not used enough sugar, not sealed well, or stored the jam in too warm a place.

If the jam crystallizes, you may have added too much sugar, stored the jars in too cold a place, or you may need more acid—add 2 tablespoons of lemon juice for every 2¼lb (1kg) fruit.

Try more Jam recipes ▶ ▶ ▶

Plum Jam with Spiced Port

6 medium jars   **45 minutes**   **9 months**

Ingredients

4lb (1.8kg) dark plums, pitted
  and cut into quarters

1 cinnamon stick, snapped in half

juice of 1 lime

6 cups granulated sugar

2–3 tbsp port, to taste

Place 1 or 2 plates in the fridge or freezer to chill.

SIMMER THE FRUIT

Put the plums, cinnamon, and lime juice into a preserving pan or a large, heavy-bottomed saucepan, then add 2 cups of water.

Why? Plums are very high in pectin and can set very quickly to a solid mass. Adding water to the fruit dilutes the pectin to a more manageable level.

Place the pan over medium heat and bring the fruit mix up to simmering point. Turn the heat down to low just as it starts to bubble, then simmer gently for 15–20 minutes or until the plums begin to break down and soften.

Remember For the freshest jam, you don't want the fruit to boil strongly at this stage, but simply to break it down to release the pectin.

BOIL TO A SET

Add the sugar to the fruit and stir with a wooden spoon until the sugar has completely dissolved. Turn the heat up high, bring to a boil, and keep at a rolling boil for 5–8 minutes or until the mixture thickens and the bubbles become large and start "plopping."

Test for a set using the wrinkle test. Take the pan off the heat. Place a teaspoon of the fruit mix on a chilled plate. Wait for a minute, then push it with your finger. If it offers resistance and wrinkles as you push it, the jam has reached the setting point. If the jam hasn't set, bring it back to a rolling boil for another minute and test again. Repeat as required.

CAN THE JAM

When the jam has set, carefully remove the cinnamon sticks, stir in the port, then ladle into warm, sterilized mason jars, leaving ¼in (5mm) headspace. Cover and seal with a two-part top, then heat process for 10 minutes (see pp.116–121). Label and store in a cool, dark place and refrigerate after opening.

Help! If the canned jam does not cool to a set, all is not lost: simply pour into a pan, bring back to a rolling boil for 1–2 minutes, and test again.

Black Currant Jam

2 small jars | **45 minutes** | **6–9 months**

Ingredients

1lb 2oz (500g) black currants, washed

3 cups granulated sugar

juice of 1 lemon

Place 1 or 2 plates in the fridge or freezer to chill.

SIMMER THE FRUIT

Put the black currants in a preserving pan or heavy saucepan and pour in 2 cups of water. Put the pan over low heat and simmer the fruit gently for 15–20 minutes.

Why? Black currants have tougher skins than many other fruits, so simmering them in water first helps to soften their skins.

BOIL TO A SET

Add the sugar and lemon juice to the pan and stir the mixture until all the sugar has dissolved—there should be no sugar crystals visible as you stir. Turn the heat up high, bring to a boil, and keep at a rapid, rolling boil for 8–10 minutes or until the mixture thickens and the bubbles become large and start "plopping."

Test for a set using the wrinkle test. Take the pan off the heat. Place a teaspoon of the fruit mixture on a chilled plate. Wait for a minute, then push it with your finger. If it offers resistance and wrinkles as you push it, the jam has reached the setting point. If the jam hasn't set, bring it back to a rolling boil for 1 more minute and test again.

Tip Black currants are high in both acid and pectin, so this jam should set quite easily and quickly.

CAN THE JAM

When you have a set, ladle into warm, sterilized mason jars, leaving ¼in (5mm) headspace. Cover, seal with a two-part top, then heat process for 10 minutes (see pp.116–121). Label and store in a cool, dark place. Once opened, keep refrigerated.

Cherry Jam

3 medium jars

45 minutes

9 months

Ingredients

1lb 2oz (500g) cherries, pits removed
and reserved

juice of 2 lemons

2¼ cups granulated sugar mixed with 1 x 0.4oz
(13g) packet of pectin

2 tbsp brandy or cherry brandy

Place 1 or 2 plates in the fridge or freezer to chill.

SIMMER THE FRUIT

Place the cherry pits in a square of cheesecloth, gather into a bag, and tie with string. Make sure the string is long enough to allow easy removal of the bag. Put the cherries along with the bag of pits into a preserving pan or a large, heavy-bottomed saucepan.

Why? You don't need to include the cherry pits, but they will add a subtle almond flavor to the jam.

Add 1¼ cups water. Place the pan over medium heat. Bring to a boil, then reduce to a simmer and cook gently for 10–15 minutes or until the cherries are tender and begin to soften. Remove the bag of pits. Pour in the lemon juice and add the sugar. Heat gently, stirring until the sugar dissolves. No sugar crystals should be visible.

Tip If you want some of the cherries to remain chunky in the jam, don't cook them for too long.

BOIL TO A SET

Turn the heat up high and bring to a boil. Keep at a steady rolling boil, stirring occasionally with a long wooden spoon, for 8–10 minutes or until it thickens.

Test for a set using the wrinkle test. Remove the pan from the heat. Place a teaspoon of the fruit mix on a chilled plate. Wait for a minute and then push it with your finger. If it offers resistance and wrinkles, the jam has reached the setting point. If the jam hasn't set, bring back to a rolling boil for another minute and test again.

CAN THE JAM

Stir in the brandy, then ladle into warm, sterilized mason jars, leaving ¼in (5mm) headspace. Cover, seal with a two-part top, then heat process for 10 minutes (see pp.116–121), and label. Refrigerate after opening.

Help! If the canned jam does not cool to a set, simply pour it into a pan, bring back to a rolling boil for 1–2 minutes, and test again.

Cherry Vodka Jam variation Replace the brandy with the same amount of plain vodka.

Rhubarb, Pear, and Ginger Jam

3 medium jars | **45 minutes** | **9 months**

Ingredients

1½lb (675g) fresh rhubarb, trimmed, rinsed, and chopped into 1in (2.5cm) pieces

2 pears, peeled, cored, and chopped

3½ cups granulated sugar

juice of 1 lemon

juice of ½ orange

2 small balls of candied ginger, finely chopped

Place 1 or 2 plates in the fridge or freezer to chill.

SIMMER THE FRUIT

Put the rhubarb and pears in a preserving pan or heavy saucepan and pour in the sugar. Put the pan over low heat and add the lemon juice, orange juice, and candied ginger. Stir until all the sugar has dissolved. No sugar crystals should be visible.

BOIL TO A SET

Turn the heat up high, bring to a boil, and keep at a rapid, rolling boil for 15–20 minutes until the mixture in the pan thickens and reaches the setting point.

Test for a set using the wrinkle test. Take the pan off the heat. Place a teaspoon of the fruit mixture on a chilled plate. Wait for a minute, then push it with your finger. If it offers resistance and wrinkles as you push it, the jam has reached the setting point.

Remember If the jam hasn't set, bring it back to a rolling boil for another minute and test again.

CAN THE JAM

When you have a set, ladle into warm, sterilized mason jars, leaving ¼in (5mm) headspace. Cover, seal with a two-part top, then heat process for 10 minutes (see pp.116–121), and label. Once opened, keep refrigerated.

Tip This jam will taste great in a pastry tart or spread as a filling over sponge cake.

How to **Make Conserve**

Making conserve involves most of the same techniques as jam, with a couple of simple differences. One is that the fruit is steeped in sugar first to firm up its skin; as you are not aiming for a strong set this means you can use riper fruit with less pectin. Secondly, conserves are boiled more gently than jam and are left to cool and thicken a little before they are canned.

Sugar begins to dissolve as it absorbs the juices of the fruit

Draw a spoon over the bottom of the pan: if it leaves a trail then the mixture has thickened sufficiently and you should test for a set

Steep in sugar

The fruit is placed in a large bowl, coated with sugar, and allowed to steep. The sugar draws out the fruit juices, drying and firming the fruit. This firming stops the fruit from breaking down completely when boiled, leaving larger chunks of fruit in the conserve.

Allow to thicken

Conserves are cooked at a steady boil—not at the same rate and intense heat as for jam. Once the conserve has set, leave it to cool a little until it has thickened. The fruit will be more evenly distributed through the liquid, and is less likely to rise to the top of the jar.

Apricot Conserve

2 medium jars

30 minutes, plus steeping

6 months

Ingredients

1lb 2oz (500g) ripe apricots

1½ cups granulated sugar (or a little less, if you prefer a softer set and fresher taste)

juice of 1 lemon

Chill a couple of plates in the fridge or freezer so that they are ready for testing the set.

STEEP THE FRUIT IN SUGAR

Halve and pit the apricots, then layer them with the sugar in a bowl. Cover the bowl with a plate and leave for several hours or overnight at room temperature.

Remember It's worth spending this extra time preparing the fruit, as the sugar firms its flesh and ensures the cooked conserve will contain large pieces of the fruit, for extra flavor and texture.

DISSOLVE THE SUGAR

Put the apricots and sugar with any juices in a preserving pan or heavy-bottomed saucepan and add the lemon juice. Put the pan over low heat and stir gently until all the sugar has dissolved.

Careful! Make sure you do not break up the fruit as you stir.

BOIL TO A SET

Turn the heat up high, bring to a boil, and keep it at a steady—not a rolling—boil for 7–10 minutes until the mix thickens and reaches the setting point. Avoid stirring the mix as you wait for a set. Take the pan off the heat and test for a set. Place a teaspoon of the mixture on a chilled plate. Wait 1 minute and then push it with your finger. If it offers

resistance and wrinkles as you push it, the mixture has set. If it does not wrinkle, bring it back to a steady boil for another minute and test again.

Remember For conserves, you are looking to achieve a relatively soft set.

CAN THE CONSERVE

Leave the conserve in the pan for a few minutes once you have a set, so the fruit can sink and distribute more evenly through the hot liquid. Ladle into clean, hot, sterilized jars, leaving ¼in (5mm) headspace. Seal with a two-part top and heat process for 5 minutes (see pp.116–121), then label. Store in a cool, dark place. All preserves, particularly ones that are made with a low amount of sugar, should be refrigerated once opened—they will all come into contact with the air when the lid is lifted.

Strawberry Conserve

3 medium jars **45 minutes, plus steeping** **6 months**

Ingredients

2lb (900g) strawberries, hulled

4 cups granulated sugar

juice of 1 lemon

juice of 1 lime

Special Equipment

cheesecloth

Place 1 or 2 plates in the fridge or freezer.

STEEP THE FRUIT IN SUGAR

Layer the strawberries with the sugar in a bowl. Cover the bowl with a plate and leave for several hours or overnight at room temperature.

DISSOLVE THE SUGAR

Put the strawberries and sugar in a preserving pan or heavy-bottomed saucepan, put the pan over low heat, and stir gently until all the sugar has dissolved.

Careful! Try not to break up the fruit as you stir.

Boil the mix gently for about 5 minutes—just until the fruit has softened but not begun to break up. Remove the pan from the heat and cover loosely with cheesecloth so the steam can escape and you aren't left with watery condensation. Set aside overnight.

BOIL TO A SET

Remove the cheesecloth, stir in the lemon and lime juice, set the pan over high heat, bring to a boil.

Why? Strawberries are low in pectin, and the citrus juices help to better release what pectin there is. The juices also provide a fresher flavor.

Boil the mixture at a steady boil, rather than rolling, for 5–10 minutes or until it thickens and reaches the setting point.

Tip Skim off any foam from the surface as the fruit boils so it doesn't affect the finished conserve.

Remove from the heat and test for the set. Place a teaspoon of the fruit mixture on a chilled plate. Wait for a minute, then push it with your finger. If it offers resistance and wrinkles as you push it, the setting point has been reached. If the mixture hasn't set, bring it back to a steady boil for 1 more minute and test again.

CAN THE CONSERVE

Leave the conserve in the pan for a few minutes once you have a set so the fruit can distribute more evenly through the hot liquid. Ladle into warm, sterilized mason jars, leaving ¼in (5mm) headspace. Cover, seal with a two-part top, then heat process for 5 minutes (see pp.116–121), and label. Store in a cool, dark place. Once opened, keep refrigerated.

Peach and Walnut Conserve

3 medium jars — **45 minutes, plus steeping** — **6 months**

Ingredients

2¾lb (1.25kg) ripe peaches

1 orange, peeled (but with pith still attached), and finely sliced

4 cups granulated sugar

juice of 1 lemon

2oz (50g) walnuts, coarsely chopped

1–2 tbsp brandy (optional)

Place 1 or 2 plates in the fridge or freezer.

PREPARE THE FRUIT

Lightly cut a cross on the top of each peach, drop it in a bowl of boiling water for 30 seconds, then transfer to a bowl of cold water. This helps to loosen the skin. Remove the peaches one by one and peel off the skin. Halve the peaches and remove and reserve all the peach pits. Coarsely chop the flesh.

Tip Choose very ripe peaches, when their flavor and scent are at their best. You can also use ripe nectarines and prepare them in the same way.

STEEP THE FRUIT IN SUGAR

Layer the peaches, sliced orange, and sugar in a large bowl. Cover the bowl with a plate and leave for 4 hours or overnight at room temperature.

Why? Setting aside the uncooked fruit for this long enables the sugar to draw out the juices, which firms up the fruit and ensures it retains more of its form and texture in soft-set conserve.

DISSOLVE THE SUGAR

Tie the peach pits in a piece of cheesecloth. Put the fruit and sugar in a preserving pan or heavy-bottomed saucepan, add the peach pits, then stir gently over low heat until the sugar has dissolved.

BOIL TO A SET

Turn the heat up high, bring to a boil, and keep it at a steady boil, rather than rolling, for 15–20 minutes or until it thickens and reaches the setting point. Take the pan off the heat and test for a set. Place a teaspoon of the fruit mixture on a chilled plate. Wait for a minute, then push it with your finger. If it offers resistance and wrinkles as you push it, the setting point has been reached. If the mixture hasn't set, bring it back to a steady boil for one more minute and test again.

CAN THE CONSERVE

Once you have a set, remove the bag of peach pits and stir in the lemon juice, walnuts, and brandy (if using). Leave the conserve in the pan for a few minutes so the fruit pieces can distribute more evenly through the hot liquid. Ladle into warm, sterilized mason jars, leaving ¼in (5mm) headspace. Cover, seal with a two-part top, then heat process for 5 minutes (see pp.116–121), and label. Store in a cool, dark place. Refrigerate the conserve after opening.

How to **Make Jelly**

Bright, translucent, jewel-like jellies are sweet preserves made from
the strained juice of simmered fruit. They are prepared in the same
way as jams, with a couple of additional stages incorporated into
the process. An important point to remember when making jelly
is that the quantity of strained juice and pectin levels always vary.

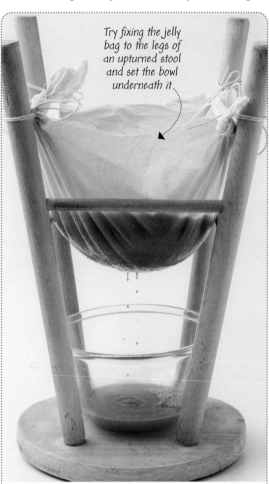

*Try fixing the jelly
bag to the legs of
an upturned stool
and set the bowl
underneath it*

*The amount of juice
collected always varies,
even with a tried-and-
tested recipe, so
calculate the correct
quantity of sugar before
you add it to the pan*

Strain the fruit

Jellies are made by straining the juice of
simmered fruit through a jelly bag (or a clean
kitchen towel or a piece of cheesecloth). For a
clear juice, be patient and let it drip through
overnight. Resist the urge to squeeze the pulp,
which will make the juice and jelly cloudy.

Calculate and add sugar

The amount of sugar required depends
on the quantity of juice, which is different
every time. Use a measuring cup to check
what you collected and work out how much
sugar to add. The usual ratio is 2 cups
of sugar for every 2 cups of juice.

Wrinkle test

Flake test

Test the jelly

Boil and test the jelly mixture as you would to make jam. Take the pan off the heat while you test for a set (see p.87). For the wrinkle test, push some jelly with your finger to see if it wrinkles. For the flake test, tilt a spoonful of jelly to see if it falls in a flat flake.

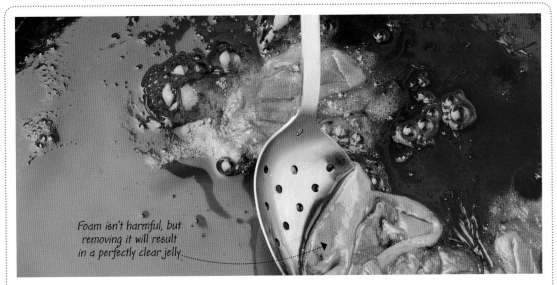

Foam isn't harmful, but removing it will result in a perfectly clear jelly.

Skim off the foam

When the jelly reaches setting point, carefully skim off any bubbly foam caused by the vigorous boil. Make sure you don't accidently stir any of the froth into a boiling mixture. Keep a bowl of warm water nearby and rinse the skimmer every time you remove foam.

Grape, Lemon, and Clove Jelly

Fruits that are juicy or high in pectin—or preferably both—
make wonderful jellies. This recipe uses red grapes, which are
high in juice but have medium pectin levels, so the addition of
a lemon helps to produce a classic delicate jelly that sets well.
Like all jellies, it is delicious with cold meats or cheeses.

3 medium jars   **1 hour plus straining**   **12 months**

Ingredients

3lb 3oz (1.5kg) underripe red grapes
(with seeds), washed and chopped
(see Tip, step 1)

1 lemon, washed and chopped

approx. 3¼ cups granulated sugar
(see method)

½ tsp cloves

red grapes

lemon

granulated sugar

cloves

Equipment

stainless steel preserving pan or large,
heavy-bottomed stainless steel saucepan

food processor (optional)

large wooden spoon

sterilized jelly bag or cheesecloth-lined
nylon strainer

sugar thermometer (optional)

wide-mouthed jam funnel (optional)

ladle

slotted spoon

sterilized jars with lids or with cellophane
covers and elastic bands

discs of waxed paper

preserving pan

wooden spoon

jam funnel

elastic bands

jelly bag

sugar thermometer

ladle   **slotted spoon**

jars

waxed paper and cellophane covers

1 Put the grapes and the lemon in a preserving pan or large, heavy-bottomed saucepan with 1¼ cups of water. Bring to a boil, cover, and cook gently for 35–40 minutes.

Tip If possible, use a food processor to chop the fruit. Finely chopped fruit requires less cooking time to soften before being strained. This results in a fruitier, fresher-tasting, clear jelly.

When the grapes soften, squish with a spoon to extract more juice

Boil-wash the jelly bag before using it so it is absolutely sterile

2 Strain the pulp through a jelly bag, or a clean nylon strainer lined with cheesecloth, set over a large clean bowl. Leave to strain overnight, or for at least 2 hours, until no more juice drips through.

Careful! Don't squeeze the jelly bag or press the pulp to extract more juice, as it may cause your jelly to become cloudy.

3 Measure the strained juice and calculate the quantity of sugar: allow 2 cups of sugar for every 2 cups of juice.

Remember The quantity of juice always varies, so work out the amount of sugar required only after measuring the juice.

Keep extra sugar on hand in case the grapes provide more juice than expected

Jelly will set when sugar reaches 220°F (105°C), but test after the minimum time given because prolonged boiling can spoil the flavor

4 Put the juice, sugar, and cloves into the pan, and bring gently to a boil, stirring to dissolve the sugar. Boil rapidly for 5–10 minutes to reach the setting point; test for a set (see p.87). Skim off any foam with a slotted spoon.

Tip Allow the mixture to cool for 5 minutes before canning to ensure the cloves don't float to the top, or remove the cloves from the hot jelly once it has reached setting point.

How to store

Ladle into warm, sterilized mason jars, cover, seal with a two-part top, then heat process (see pp.116–121), and label. Store your jars in a cool, dark place. They will keep for approximately 9–12 months.

Refrigerate opened jars of jelly and use within 3–4 weeks.

Did anything go wrong?

The jelly won't set, or turns very dark. You may have boiled it for too long. Prolonged boiling is detrimental to pectin and may mean the jelly will not set and will turn darker the longer it is boiled. The pectin content of fruit varies, so to ensure there is sufficient pectin to achieve a set, simmer the fruit with a chopped lemon and use jelly sugar with added pectin (see p.89).

Try other fruits and combinations

Good choices include red currants; black currants; strawberries—but add a chopped lemon because they vary in pectin; blackberries with apple and cinnamon; and quinces.

Apple jellies also make a good basis for herb jellies, such as rosemary and sage. Tart apples have the most pectin.

Try more Jelly recipes ▶ ▶ ▶

Cranberry Jelly

2 small jars

1¼ hours, plus straining

6–9 months

Ingredients

1lb 2oz (500g) fresh or frozen cranberries

1 tbsp lemon juice

approx. 2¼ cups granulated sugar
   (see method)

Place 1 or 2 small plates in the fridge to chill.

EXTRACT THE JUICE

Put the berries in a preserving pan or large, heavy-bottomed saucepan with 2 cups water and the lemon juice. Put the pan over medium heat and bring to a boil. Turn the heat down, cover, and simmer for 25–30 minutes until the cranberries are tender.

Mash the cooked berries with a fork or masher. Pour into a sterilized jelly bag or cheesecloth-lined strainer, set over a bowl, and let strain overnight.

BOIL TO A SET

Measure the juice and work out the correct amount of sugar: allow 2 cups of sugar for every 2 cups of juice.

Why? You need to recalcuate the sugar quantities each time you make the jelly because it's impossible to predict precisely how much juice the cranberries will yield.

Pour the juice into the preserving pan, add the sugar, and stir over low heat until the sugar has dissolved. Turn the heat up high, bring to a boil, and keep it at a steady boil, rather than rolling, for 10–15 minutes until the mix thickens and reaches the setting point.

Take the pan off the heat and do a wrinkle test to check for a set. Place a teaspoon of the fruit

mixture on a chilled plate. Wait for a minute, then push it with your finger. If it offers resistance and wrinkles as you push it, the setting point has been reached. If the mixture hasn't set, bring it back to a rolling boil for 1 minute and test again.

CAN THE JELLY

Skim off any foam when you have a set, ladle into warm, sterilized jars, leaving ¼in (5mm) headspace. Seal with a two-part top and heat process for 5 minutes (see pp.116–121), then label. Store in a cool, dark place. Once opened, refrigerate and eat within 3 weeks.

Rosemary Jelly

6 medium jars

1½ hours, plus straining

9 months

Ingredients

a large handful of rosemary sprigs

2lb (900g) tart apples, coarsely chopped and with the core and seeds retained

approx. 4 cups granulated sugar (see method)

juice of 1 lemon

Place 1 or 2 small plates in the fridge to chill.

OVEN-DRY THE ROSEMARY

Preheat the oven to 300°F (150°C). Strip the rosemary leaves from their stems and scatter onto a baking sheet. Reserve the stems. Oven-dry the leaves for 30–40 minutes, then set aside to cool.

EXTRACT THE JUICE

Put the chopped apples, and their cores and seeds, in a preserving pan or large, heavy-bottomed saucepan with 4 cups of water. Add the rosemary stems. Put the pan over medium heat, bring to a boil, then simmer for 30–40 minutes until the apples are soft and mushy.

Why? Apple cores contain high levels of pectin to help achieve a good set and the rosemary stems add flavor. Both can be added without affecting the texture of the jelly because the pulp is discarded after straining.

Break up the apples, if needed, with a fork or potato masher. Pour the pulp into a sterilized jelly bag, or a cheesecloth-lined strainer, set over a bowl. Let strain, ideally overnight.

BOIL TO A SET

Measure the juice and calculate the sugar needed: allow 2 cups of sugar for every 2 cups of juice. Pour the juice, sugar, lemon juice, and

oven-dried rosemary leaves in the pan and stir over low heat until the sugar has dissolved.

Turn the heat up high, bring to a boil, and keep it at a rolling boil for 20 minutes, until the juice thickens and reaches the setting point.

Take the pan off the heat and test for a set using the wrinkle test. Place a teaspoon of the fruit mixture on a chilled plate. Wait for a minute, then push it with your finger. If it offers resistance and wrinkles as you push it, the setting point has been reached. If the mixture hasn't set, bring it back to a rolling boil for 1 minute and test again.

CAN THE JELLY

Skim off any foam that has formed on the surface when you have a set, and stir well.

Remember Leave the jelly for 10 minutes for the rosemary leaves to sink below the surface and distribute themselves evenly through the jelly.

Ladle into warm, sterilized mason jars. Cover, seal with a two-part top, then heat process for 5 minutes (see pp.116–121), and label. Store in a cool, dark place. Once opened, keep refrigerated and consume within 3 weeks.

How to **Make Syrups and Cordials**

Preserving seasonal produce as homemade syrups and cordials is
a wonderful way to enjoy its fruity flavors at any time of year. The
techniques of cooking the fruit, straining the juices, and sweetening
and preserving with sugar are easy to master.

Use refined white granulated sugar so it does not mask the flavor of the juice

Check the quantity of strained juice in a measuring cup

Simmer and strain the fruit

For the best flavor, use minimal amounts of
water to simmer. Soft fruits like strawberries
only need a thin film, but for thick-skinned
fruits like black currants use ⅔ cup of water
for every 2 cups of fruit. Strain the pulp,
pressing gently to extract all the juice.

Sweeten the juice

Measure the juice to calculate the amount of
sugar. Every 2 cups of juice needs 1½ cups
of sugar. Stir until the sugar has dissolved,
then add 1 teaspoon of citric acid (vitamin C
powder) to inhibit the growth of bacteria
and prevent discoloration.

Use a sterilized long-spouted funnel to bottle the sweetened juice ......▶

...... Use sterilized bottles with swing stopper lids for cordials and syrups ▶

Tip Homemade syrups are extremely versatile ingredients. Dilute them with still or sparkling water to create refreshing drinks, or use them to add delicious flavors to ice creams, milkshakes, fruit salads, or smoothies.

Bottle the liquid

When the sugar has completely dissolved, pour the liquid immediately into warm sterilized bottles with the help of a sterilized funnel, or pour it into containers to freeze, leaving 1in (2.5cm) of space at the top of each container to allow for expansion.

Blackberry Syrup

2 small bottles   **25 minutes**   **1–2 months**

Ingredients

1lb (450g) ripe blackberries or loganberries

approx. 1½ cups granulated sugar (see method)

1 tsp citric or ascorbic acid (vitamin C powder)

Special Equipment

large saucepan

sterilized jelly bag, or cheesecloth and a fine strainer

mixing bowl

measuring cup

sterilized long-necked funnel

sterilized bottles

EXTRACT THE JUICE

Heat the blackberries in a saucepan with a little water—just enough to cover the bottom of the pan. Simmer over low heat for a short time until the juices run, about 3–5 minutes. Crush the fruit with the back of a wooden spoon or a potato masher as it simmers.

Careful! Heat the fruit very gently over low heat to preserve as much of the juice's nutritional content and flavor as possible.

STRAIN THE PULP

Transfer the pulp to a jelly bag or a cheesecloth-lined strainer set over a bowl.

Careful! Press the pulp gently with a spoon to release the last of the juice. The gentle pressure ensures that the juice does not become clouded with pieces of pulp.

Pour the juice into a measuring cup and calculate the amount of sugar you will need. For every 2 cups of juice, use 1½ cups of sugar. Add the sugar and the citric acid to the juice and stir until the sugar has completely dissolved.

POUR INTO BOTTLES

When all the sugar has dissolved, pour the syrup into bottles using the funnel. Seal the bottles, let cool, label, and store in the fridge.

Remember If you want to keep the syrup for longer, you can pour it into freezer jars and store in the freezer for up to 6 months until you need it. Make sure you leave 1in (2.5cm) at the top of each jar for the liquid to expand as it freezes.

Strawberry Syrup

2 small bottles

25–35 minutes

1–2 months

Ingredients

1lb (450g) strawberries, hulled and sliced

1 tbsp lemon juice

1 vanilla bean, split, with seeds scraped out and reserved, or 1 tsp vanilla extract

¾–1 cup granulated sugar (see method)

1 tsp citric or ascorbic acid (vitamin C powder)

Special Equipment

large saucepan

sterilized jelly bag, or cheesecloth and a fine strainer

mixing bowl

measuring cup

sterilized long-necked funnel

sterilized bottles

EXTRACT THE JUICE

Heat the strawberries in a saucepan with approximately ¾ cup water. Simmer over low heat for a short time until the juices run. Crush the fruit with the back of a wooden spoon or a potato masher as it cooks.

Remember The delicate skins of strawberries willingly release their juice, so make sure you only just cover them with a film of water to avoid diluting the juice more than necessary, or losing too much flavor.

STRAIN THE PULP

Pour the pulp into a jelly bag or cheesecloth-lined strainer set over a bowl. Press the pulp gently with a spoon to release the last of the juice.

Pour the juice into a measuring cup and work out how much sugar to use. For every ½ cup of juice, use ⅓ cup of sugar.

COOK THE SYRUP

Clean out the pan and pour the juice back into it. Add the sugar and vanilla bean, and whisk in the vanilla seeds. Set the pan over low heat and cook gently, without stirring, until the sugar has completely dissolved and the crystals are no longer visible. Bring to a boil and simmer for 5 minutes.

POUR INTO BOTTLES

Take the pan off the heat, remove the vanilla bean and discard, and stir in the citric acid. Pour the syrup into bottles using a funnel. Seal the bottles, let cool, label, then store in the fridge.

Serve with sliced strawberries—or if you're feeling decadent, try adding it to champagne or sparkling wine to make a dazzling aperitif.

Raspberry and Vanilla Syrup variation
Replace the strawberries with raspberries, use 1 cup of granulated sugar, and omit the lemon juice. There's no need to scrape out the vanilla seeds—just put the whole split bean into the juice and cook over low heat without stirring until the sugar dissolves.

Fresh Mint Cordial

1 small bottle

2½–3 hours

1 month, refrigerated

Ingredients

1¾–3½oz (50–100g) peppermint, Moroccan mint, or spearmint (garden mint) leaves (see Tip)

1¼ cups granulated sugar

a few drops of natural green food coloring (optional)

a few drops of natural peppermint extract (if using spearmint)

Special Equipment

large bowl

fine strainer

large saucepan

sterilized long-necked funnel

sterilized bottle

MAKE A PASTE

Put the mint leaves and sugar in a large bowl and crush them into a paste using the end of a rolling pin or the pestle from a mortar and pestle.

Tip This quantity of mint leaves gives a delicate flavor; if you prefer a more powerful punch, use double the amount of leaves.

Pour 1¼ cups of boiling water into the bowl and stir to combine. Cover the bowl and leave for at least 2 hours, or until the water has cooled and the flavors have infused.

COOK THE CORDIAL

Set a strainer over a saucepan and strain the mixture into the pan. Press the leaves to extract the last of the juice. Cook the mix over medium heat, stirring until the sugar has dissolved, then turn up the heat and boil for 2 minutes.

POUR INTO BOTTLES

Remove the pan from the heat and stir in the food coloring and peppermint extract, if using. Pour the syrup into a bottle using the funnel. Seal the bottles, let cool, and label. Store in the fridge.

Tip You can serve this cordial diluted with still or sparkling water, or mix it with vodka and ice for a refreshing cocktail.

Black Currant Cordial

1 large bottle   **20 minutes**   **6–8 weeks**

Ingredients

1lb (450g) black currants

1 cup sugar

zest and juice of 1 lemon

Special Equipment

large saucepan

cheesecloth

sterilized long-necked funnel

sterilized bottle

MAKE THE JUICE

Put the black currants, sugar, and 1 cup water in a saucepan and cook over low heat, stirring until the sugar has dissolved.

Simmer over low heat for 5–8 minutes until the juices from the black currants start to run.

Remember To extract the maximum amount of juice, use the back of a wooden spoon or a potato masher to gently crush the fruit as it cooks.

POUR INTO A BOTTLE

Remove the pan from the heat, stir in the lemon juice, then strain the liquid through a funnel lined with cheesecloth into a bottle.

Why? The cheesecloth captures the black currant skins and ensures that the juice is beautifully clear.

Seal the bottle, let cool, label, and store in the fridge.

Tip For a thirst-quenching drink full of fizz, dilute 2 tablespoons of cordial with chilled sparkling water, and enjoy!

How to **Can Fruit in Syrup**

Canning is a great way to prolong the harvest, providing sophisticated desserts at any time of year. The fruit is packed into jars, covered in syrup, and then boiled in the jar (heat processed) to remove both bacteria and air. This results in a strong vacuum seal that allows long storage times.

Tip You can add extra flavor to the syrup with whole spices such as cinnamon, cloves, a vanilla bean, or even fresh leaves like lavender, mint, or scented geranium. Add with the sugar and remove when the syrup is ready (see p.57 for how to make a spice bag).

Making sugar syrup

Sugar syrup keeps the flavor and texture of canned fruit as intact as possible—and sometimes improves the flavor! Boil sugar and water in a pan over low heat for 1–2 minutes, stirring to dissolve all the sugar so there are no grainy bits. For every 2 cups water, use ½ cup sugar for a light syrup, ⅔ cup for medium, and 1¼ cups for heavy.

Packing the fruit

Cut the fruit into halves or quarters and pack into warm, sterilized jars. Pour in the syrup up to the brim. For screw-top jars, fit a new rubber ring seal, screw on the lid, then release it by a quarter turn. For clip jars, fit the rubber ring onto the lid and clamp the lid down. The rubber ring separates the top of the jar and the lid so air can escape when it's heated.

Leave a ½in (1cm) gap above the fruit so it will be submerged in the syrup

Use screw-top (mason) jars: they are stronger and their seals allow air to exit when heat processing

Heat processing the screw-top (mason) jars

Place a folded kitchen towel or trivet in the bottom of a large stainless-steel pan and put the jars on top; the jars will crack if placed directly on the base of the pan. Wrap the jars with kitchen towels to ensure they don't touch. Fill the pan with enough warm water to come 1in (2.5cm) above the jars. Cover the pan and bring slowly to a simmer, then heat for the required time (see table). Use tongs to remove the jars and immediately tighten the clips or screw-top lids. Test the seals 24 hours after heat processing. Try to pry off each lid with one fingernail. If it remains firmly in place, the seal is airtight and the jar is safe to store.

Water-bath Heat Processing Times

To ensure all the air is evacuated, the jars and their contents must be heated through completely. Heat processing times therefore vary according to the contents of the jar. This table provides typical simmering times for popular fruits, assuming a starting temperature of the water of 100°F (38°C), and that it reaches a simmering point of 190°F (88°C) in 25–30 minutes. Use a sugar thermometer to gauge the correct temperatures.

Fruit	Heat processing time (minutes)
Apples (sliced)	2
Apricots (halved/sliced)	10
Blackberries (whole)	2
Black currants (whole)	2
Blueberries (whole)	2
Boysenberries (whole)	2
Cherries (whole)	10
Citrus fruits (sections)	10
Cranberries (whole)	2
Figs (with lemon juice)	60–70
Gooseberries (whole)	10
Kumquats	10
Loganberries (whole)	2
Mulberries (whole)	2
Nectarines and peaches (halved/sliced)	20
Pears (halved/sliced)	40
Plums, all types (halved/sliced)	20
Quinces (sliced)	30
Raspberries (whole)	2
Red and white currants (whole)	2
Rhubarb (stewed)	10
Strawberries (whole/sliced)	2
Tayberries (whole)	2

Peaches in Syrup

Peaches canned in syrup make a glorious preserve that can be enjoyed long after the peach season is over. Like most fruits, peaches can well and require minimal preparation before being heat processed to preserve them for several months.

2 small jars

15 minutes plus heat processing

12 months if heat processed

Ingredients

½–1¼ cups granulated sugar (see method)

4–5 just-ripe peaches

Equipment

saucepan

sharp knife

cutting board

screw-top or clip jars with lids and new rubber seals

ladle

stainless steel preserving pan

kitchen towels or trivet

tongs

granulated sugar   **peaches**

sharp knife

saucepan

cutting board

screw-top jars

ladle   **preserving pan**   **kitchen towels**   **tongs**

1 To make the syrup, put the sugar in a pan, add 2 cups of water, bring gently to a boil, and boil for 1–2 minutes.

Remember Choose a light, medium, or heavy syrup depending on how tart the fruit is, or how sweet you want it to taste (see p.116). It won't affect the longevity of the preserve, but it does dictate the amount of sugar you need to use.

Use the approriate amount of sugar for the "weight" of the syrup you intend to create

Handle the fruit as little as possible so it doesn't bruise

2 Peel the peaches, cut them in half, and carefully remove the pits. Reserve a few peach pits if you want to use the kernels to add a slightly bitter almond flavor.

Help! If the peach skins don't peel off easily, dip them in a bowl of boiling water for 30 seconds and try peeling the skins again.

3 Pack the peach halves into warm sterilized screw-top jars, leaving a gap of ½in (1cm) at the top. Crack the peach pits with a nutcracker or clean pair of pliers to obtain the kernels, if using, and add with the peaches. Fill each jar with the hot syrup, ensuring the peaches are completely covered.

Tip Place the empty jars on a sheet of newspaper before filling to catch any syrup drips or spills.

Carefully pack the fruit as tightly as possible without bruising it, as it will shrink during heat processing

After sealing the lids, turn them back a quarter-turn to ensure air can escape

4 Tap the filled jars gently on the work surface and swivel them to remove any air bubbles. Fit the lids firmly—but remember to loosen them enough to allow air to evacuate during processing. Heat process the jars in a water bath (see p.117 for timings). Carefully remove the jars and tighten the lids immediately.

5 Leave the bottled fruits for 24 hours, then test each seal. If the seal is airtight (see p.117), refasten the lid and store the jar.

Tip If you use screw-top jars with metal lids, the slightly concave lid and lack of "give" once pressed indicates that you have a seal. You can test clip jars by releasing the catch and upturning them over a bowl: the vacuum should hold the lid—and its contents—in place.

Try to gently pry off the lid with your fingertip

How to store

Label and store the heat-processed jars in a cool, dark place, where they will keep for up to 12 months. Once you have opened a jar, store it in the fridge and use it within 2 weeks.

Did anything go wrong?

The lid lifts easily when you test the seal. The heat processing was not successful; it has failed to evacuate all the air from the jar to create the necessary vacuum to preserve the fruit. The good news is that although it won't keep for long, you can still eat the contents. Store in the fridge and eat within 2 weeks.

Try other fruits

Good fruits to can include greengage plums, plums, pears, nectarines, raspberries, and blueberries.

Make sure the fruit you choose for canning is firm, fresh, and without any discoloration, blemishes, or bruises.

Try more Canned Fruit recipes ▶ ▶ ▶

Figs in Honey Syrup

2 small jars

1 hour, plus heat processing

12 months if heat processed

Ingredients

1 cup honey

2 thinly peeled strips of washed lemon zest (about ½in/1cm wide)

juice of 1 lemon (approx. 2 tbsp)

approx. 16 small ripe figs, or 12 large figs, washed and dried

PREPARE THE FIGS

Cook the honey, lemon zest and juice, and 2 cups of water in a saucepan over low heat, stirring until the honey has dissolved. Bring the mix to a boil and boil for 3 minutes.

Carefully lower the figs into a boiling syrup and boil for another 2 minutes.

PACK THE JARS

Using a slotted spoon, transfer the figs from the pan to warm, sterilized screw-top or rubber seal preserving jars.

Careful! Don't squish the figs too much as you fill the jars, or they may split and lose their shape.

Remove and discard the zest from the syrup. Pour the syrup into the jars to completely cover the figs. Tap each jar gently on the work surface to release any air bubbles in the syrup. Fit the metal lids or rubber bands and seal the jars. If you are using screw-top jars, loosen the lids by a quarter turn.

HEAT PROCESS THE JARS

Put a kitchen towel or trivet in the bottom of a preserving pan or large, heavy-bottomed saucepan. Wrap the jars with kitchen towels to ensure they don't knock against each other during heat

processing, and place them in the pan. Fill the pan with enough warm water to cover the jars by 1in (2.5cm), then cover the pan and bring slowly to a simmer. Heat for the required time (see p.117).

SEAL, TEST, AND STORE

Remove the jars with tongs and tighten the lids if using screw-top jars.

Careful! Use a kitchen towel to protect your hands from the heat of the jars as you tighten the lids.

Leave the jars to cool for 24 hours before testing the seals. If the seal is airtight, you can refasten the lids and store the jars in a cool, dark place. Refrigerate after opening and use within 2 weeks.

Remember If heat processing has failed to create a strong vacuum seal, you can still enjoy the flavored fruit and syrup: treat it as an opened jar and consume within 2 weeks.

Clementines in Caramel Syrup

1 large jar | **25 minutes, plus heat processing** | **12 months if heat processed**

Ingredients

⅔ cup granulated sugar

10 small clementines, peeled, white pith scraped off with a knife

MAKE THE SYRUP

Put the sugar and ½ cup cold water in a saucepan and stir well. Heat gently without stirring until the sugar has dissolved.

Turn up the heat and boil rapidly for 5–8 minutes or until the syrup becomes a golden caramel color. Pour in 1 cup hot water. Stir until the caramel has dissolved and bring back to a boil.

Careful! The boiling caramel syrup will tend to spit as you stir it, so protect your hand with a kitchen towel or cloth.

PACK THE JARS

Place the fruits in a warm, sterilized screw-top or rubber seal preserving jar, leaving ½in (1cm) of space at the top. Pour the syrup into the jar to cover the clementines completely. Tap the jar gently on a work surface to release any air bubbles in the syrup. Fit the metal lid or rubber band and seal the jar. If you are using a screw-top jar, loosen the lid by a quarter turn.

HEAT PROCESS THE JARS

Put a kitchen towel or trivet in the bottom of a preserving pan or heavy-bottomed saucepan. Wrap the jar in a kitchen towel for extra protection and place it in the pan. Fill the pan with enough warm water to cover the jar by 1in (2.5cm), then cover the pan and bring slowly to a simmer. Heat for the required time for citrus fruits (see p.117).

SEAL, TEST, AND STORE

Remove the jar with tongs and tighten the lid if using a screw-top jar.

Careful! Use a kitchen towel to protect your hands from the heat of the jar as you tighten the lid.

Leave the jar to cool for 24 hours, then test the seal. If the seal is airtight, you can refasten the lid and store the jar in a cool, dark place. Refrigerate after opening and use within 2 weeks.

Remember If heat processing has failed to create a strong vacuum seal, you can still enjoy the fruit and caramel syrup: treat it as an opened jar and consume within 2 weeks.

How to **Dry Fruit and Vegetables**

Dehydration is one of the oldest-known methods of food preservation, probably because it is so simple and extremely effective: it draws out all the moisture that unwanted microorganisms, such as bacteria and mold, require to survive. The only thing you need in abundance is time, as it takes many hours to dry the produce properly.

Air-dry flat

Leave small items, such as little mushrooms, whole

The produce is ready when it has shriveled to about half its original size, but is still pliable

PREPARE THE PRODUCE

Air-drying is a slow process, but placing the produce near a heat source speeds up the evaporation. Slice fresh fruit or vegetables thinly into small pieces. Arrange on baking sheets or wire racks lined with paper towels. Ensure no pieces overlap or touch each other.

DRY OVER A SOURCE OF HEAT

Place the sheets or racks 2–4in (5–10cm) above a heat source, such as on a wood-burning stove, radiator, or in a warm airing cupboard, and leave overnight. When the produce has dried, remove from the heat source, but leave on the sheet until completely cold.

Air-dry hanging up

You can also dry orange and lemon peel by hanging up

Hang the herb bundles at regular intervals

Oven-dry

The dried produce will look and feel like soft, pliable chamois leather

Turn the slices occasionally as they dry

Tip To dry fruit like pears and apples that brown quickly once cut, drop the fruit slices into a large bowl of water mixed with a little lemon juice for a few seconds. Drain and dry them on a kitchen towel, then arrange on the wire racks to dry.

Air can circulate easily around produce like herbs if they are hung up to air-dry. Tie the herbs into bundles with kitchen string and hang from a piece of thick string tied across an airy, dry room and away from direct sunlight. Leave the herbs for at least 2 weeks to dry thoroughly.

Slice fruit or vegetables into small pieces ¼–½in (5mm–1cm) thick. Arrange in a single layer on wire racks set over baking sheets. Place in an oven set at its lowest temperature of 120–140°F (50–60°C), for up to 24 hours. Leave the oven slightly ajar, using a skewer, to create an airflow.

Oven-dried Tomatoes

Drying tomatoes in the oven is an easy way of achieving the same intense, rich flavor of sun-dried tomatoes, now a commonplace ingredient in modern cooking. With tomatoes so abundant in season, oven-drying makes a great way of using up spare produce.

| 3 medium jars | 10 minutes plus drying | 2 weeks (12 months if frozen) |

Ingredients

6½lb (3kg) ripe, firm,
    medium-sized tomatoes

2–3 tsp salt

olive oil to cover (optional)

Equipment

sharp knife

cutting board

wire racks

baking sheets

sterilized jars with lids

tomatoes　　　　**salt**

airtight jars with lids　　　　**olive oil**

wire racks

cutting board

sharp knife

baking sheets

1 Check the tomatoes and remove any that are blemished or bruised. Use a sharp knife to cut round tomatoes in half horizontally and plum tomatoes vertically. Score a cross in each half with a sharp knife and push up the center.

Why? Pushing up the center of each scored tomato helps to expose more of the flesh to the drying air.

Push up the center of the tomatoes with your fingertips

Just a pinch of salt will be enough to start drawing out moisture

2 Arrange the tomatoes with their crossed sides facing up on wire racks set over baking sheets. Sprinkle each lightly with salt and leave for a few minutes. Then turn the halves over, making sure that the tomatoes are not touching each other.

Why? Sprinkling the tomatoes with salt helps to start drawing out moisture. The baking sheets will catch all the juice.

3 Put the sheets in the oven on a low setting, 150–175°F (60–80°C), and dry for 8–12 hours, checking regularly to ensure they are not burning. When the tomatoes are dry, remove from the oven and let cool on the racks.

Tip Prop the oven door open very slightly by inserting a skewer between the frame and the door, to ensure the tomatoes dry out rather than cook.

Dried tomatoes should leave no residue when pressed in the center

4 Pack the tomatoes into sterilized jars, either dry or completely covered in olive oil so they become softer. If storing in oil, tap the jars gently on the work surface to remove any air pockets.

Why? Tomatoes in oil are softer and less chewy than dry ones. This makes them more suitable for salads or as an antipasto, as they can be eaten straight from the fridge.

Cover the tomatoes completely with the oil

How to store

Keep the packed tomato jars in the fridge and use within 2 weeks.

To store the dried tomatoes for longer, freeze on open baking sheets, pack them into small freezer bags, and freeze for up to 12 months. To use, allow the tomatoes to thaw, then pack them into a sterilized jar and pour in olive oil to cover completely, if preferred. Store in the fridge and use within one week.

Did anything go wrong?

If the tomatoes taste slightly toasted or look burnt around the edges, they may have become moldy. Throw the produce away and, next time, make sure to keep the oven on its lowest setting and check the tomatoes regularly.

If the tomatoes have a slightly metallic taste to them, next time cover the wire racks with a cheesecloth before you arrange the tomato halves on them.

Try other vegetables

Try drying thinly sliced beets, carrots, and parsnips to make vegetable crisps.

Try drying more fruit and vegetables ▶ ▶ ▶

Dried Mushrooms

2 small jars **15 minutes, plus drying** **9–12 months (12 months if frozen)**

Ingredients

1lb (450g) chestnut, shiitake, or buna-shimeji
   mushrooms, or freshly picked wild mushrooms

PREPARE THE MUSHROOMS

Thickly slice large mushrooms and leave small
ones whole. Lay some paper towels over wire racks
and arrange the mushrooms on top, making sure
none of them overlap.

LET DRY

Place the racks of mushrooms 2–4in (5–10cm)
above a wood-burning stove, radiator, boiler, Aga,
night storage heater, or warm airing cupboard
and leave overnight. Alternatively, place the racks
in the oven on its lowest setting—120–140°F
(50–60°C)—for several hours.

Tip Prop the oven door open slightly with a skewer
to ensure it doesn't get too hot and to keep the
air circulating.

The mushrooms are dried when they have
shrunk to half their size, but are still pliable. Store
the dried mushrooms in glass jars in a cool, dark
place. Alternatively, freeze on open trays, pack into
freezer bags or containers, and store in the freezer.

Careful! Make sure the mushrooms are
completely cold before you put them in glass jars.
Any steam trapped inside will condense, creating
a damp environment and causing the mushrooms
to deteriorate.

Tip Add a few grains of rice to each jar to help the
mushrooms stay as dry as possible. The grains act
as a desiccant, absorbing any trapped moisture.

Dried Apples

2 small jars | **15–20 minutes plus drying** | **6 months (12 months if frozen)**

Ingredients

2 tbsp lemon juice or ½ tsp citric or ascorbic acid (vitamin C powder)

2¼lb (1kg) ripe apples, washed, cored, and sliced into ⅛–¼in (3–5mm) thick rings

PREPARE THE APPLE RINGS

Pour 2 cups of water into a bowl, add the lemon juice or citric or ascorbic acid, and stir. Drop a small batch of apple rings into the water, lift them out, drain on a kitchen towel, and arrange on wire racks, making sure they don't overlap.

Why? Dipping the apple slices in acidulated water prevents them from browning.

Place the racks in the oven on its lowest setting 120–140°F (50–60°C) for 8–24 hours, depending on the temperature. Turn the slices occasionally as they dry.

Help! If the prospect of drying apple rings for such a long time seems daunting, you can dry them in stages over several days if you prefer.

STORE IN JARS

The apple rings are ready when they have shrunk, are pliable, and feel like soft chamois leather. Take them out of the oven, cover with paper towels, and leave for 12–24 hours. Turn often as they cool to evaporate as much moisture as possible.

Pack the dried rings into airtight jars and store in a cool, dark place. Make sure they are completely cold before you do this. If freezing, freeze the dried apples on open trays, then pack into freezer bags and store in the freezer.

Careful! Check the dried rings regularly for any signs of mold or deterioration and discard any that aren't in perfect condition.

Try other fruits

Pitted fruits For drying pitted fruits such as apricots, halve the fruits, remove the pits, and dry the halves cut-side up.

Thick-rind fruits For fruits with thick rind or peel such as melons and bananas, remove the rind or peel first and take out any seeds.

Thin-skin fruits Dip fruits with thin skins such as grapes into boiling water for 30 seconds to split the skins. Then drain, pat dry, and oven-dry.

Large fruits Larger fruits such as peaches and figs should be dried by cutting in half and drying cut-side up.

3
Take It Further

Now that you have mastered some of the most valuable preserving skills, it's time to become more adventurous. This chapter covers a range of more unusual recipes that broaden the horizons of the home-preserver. Why rely on store-bought when you can learn the art of curing, try your hand at butter- and cheese-making, and even brew your own alcohol?

In this section, learn to prepare or make:

Marmalade
pp.134–141

Fruit Curd
pp.142–149

Butter
pp.150–155

Soft Cheese
pp.156–157

Alcoholic Drinks
pp.158–165

Dry- and Wet-cured Fish
pp.166–173

Wet- and Dry-cured Meat
pp.174–183

Potted Meats
pp.184–187

How to **Make Marmalade**

Marmalade—a gelled fruit spread, like jam—is always made with citrus fruit, which gives it its unique tangy flavor. Preparing marmalade builds on your technical knowledge of jam-making by incorporating a straightforward stage of cooking the hard peel slowly for a time to soften it first before adding the sugar.

The citrus shells should feel softened if you test them with a wooden spoon

Tip Make sure the peel is soft enough before combining with the sugar, as sugar prevents any further softening.

Boiling shells, pith, and seeds

To soften the peel, and to extract maximum pectin, which is concentrated in the peel, pith, and seeds, put the seeds and any spare pith in a cheesecloth bag (see p.57). Place the bag, along with the shells, in a pan of water, half-cover, and boil for 1 hour or until the shells are soft.

Cut the soft peel into short shreds

Cutting the peel

Allow the citrus shells to cool. Once they are cool enough to handle, use a sharp knife to cut the cooked citrus shells into evenly sliced strands on a cutting board. Chop the strands into thin, medium, or thick shreds depending on how you like your marmalade.

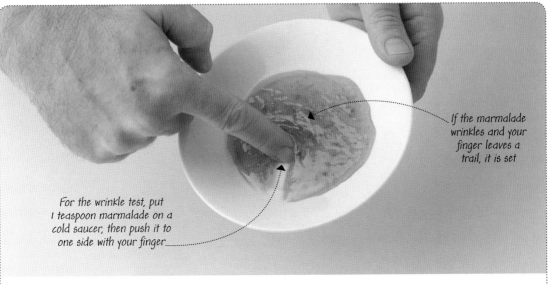

If the marmalade wrinkles and your finger leaves a trail, it is set

For the wrinkle test, put 1 teaspoon marmalade on a cold saucer, then push it to one side with your finger

Wrinkle test and flake test

Marmalades usually take 5–20 minutes boiling time to set, depending on how much pectin the batch contains. There are two set tests: a flake test and a wrinkle test. For the flake test, tilt 1 teaspoon marmalade. If the last of the mixture falls in a flat flake rather than a stream, it is set.

Practice MAKING MARMALADE

Orange Marmalade

Like jam, preparing this classic, bittersweet preserve is
a systematic process. The citrus peel must be prepared
before boiling the marmalade for a set. Marmalade is not
just for breakfast; use it as a glaze for oven-baked ham (see
p.183), as a topping, with desserts, or as a filling for cakes.

2 small jars   1¾–2 hours   12 months

sweet oranges   lemons   granulated sugar

Ingredients

2¼lb (1kg) large sweet oranges,
   scrubbed and stems removed
   (or see variation below)

2 lemons, unwaxed

4½ cups granulated sugar

sharp knife

cutting board   string   cheesecloth

Equipment

sharp knife

cutting board

cheesecloth

string

preserving pan or large,
   heavy-bottomed saucepan

large wooden spoon

sugar thermometer

wide-mouthed jam funnel

ladle

slotted spoon (optional)

jars with lids or with cellophane
   covers and elastic bands

discs of waxed paper

**wooden spoon   sugar
                   thermometer**

preserving pan

Seville Marmalade variation

Replace the large, sweet oranges with small, bitter Seville oranges. They have a thick, rough skin, tart flesh, and lots of seeds, which makes them high enough in pectin to give a well-set marmalade. Use the same quantity of Seville oranges, 1 lemon, and 5 cups of granulated sugar.

jam funnel   ladle   slotted spoon

jars

**discs of waxed
paper and
cellophane covers**

**elastic
bands**

1 Place one or two plates in the fridge or freezer to cool. Halve the oranges and lemons, squeeze their juice into a measuring cup, and reserve it in the fridge so it stays fresh. Collect the pith and seeds from the juicer, place them in a square of cheesecloth, and tie into a bundle.

Tip Tie the cheesecloth with a long string to make it easy to remove from the pan.

Cheesecloth contains the seeds and pith, but releases their pectin

Reserve all the liquor from boiling the shells

2 Put the citrus shells in a preserving pan or large, heavy-bottomed saucepan, add the cheesecloth bag and 4 cups of water. Bring to a boil, then simmer for 1 hour or until soft. Pour the ingredients into a large colander set over a bowl. Scoop out the rest of the pith to leave the peel. Reserve the pith and liquid.

Tip Press the shells lightly to extract as much liquid as possible.

3 Cut the peel into short strands. Add some of the lemon peel for variety. Put the sliced peel, reserved liquid, and juice in the saucepan. Add the sugar and heat gently, stirring until it has dissolved. Boil rapidly for 5–20 minutes or until a set is achieved. Remove the pan from the heat while you test for a set (see p.135).

Remember Shorter boiling makes fresher marmalade, so test early.

Start testing for set early and retest every 2–3 minutes until you get a set

4 Once the marmalade has set, leave it for 10–12 minutes to cool and thicken slightly, so the strands will be evenly distributed. Skim off any foam, ladle into warm, sterilized jars, leaving ¼in (5mm) headspace. Cover, seal with a two-part top, heat process for 10 minutes (see pp.116–121), and label.

Careful! Don't let the marmalade cool too much—can it while still above 185°F (85°C).

Use sterilized equipment (see p.11) to can the preserve

Can before the marmalade cools too much to keep the sterilization process intact and to ensure the preserve won't spoil once canned

How to store

Label the jars and store them in a cool dark place for up to 12 months.

Did anything go wrong?

If the marmalade tastes peculiar or won't set, it may be that you have boiled it for too long; prolonged boiling affects both flavor and set.

If your peel is tough and hard, make sure you cook the citrus shells longer next time, as sugar hardens the peel. Alternatively, adding a lemon should help to overcome this problem.

Further tips

Although the basic method of making marmalade is the same, different recipes may require different quantities of sugar, depending on whether the fruit is bitter, tangy, or sweet.

Look for ripe citrus fruits with no blemishes or bruises for a superior-tasting marmalade. Don't choose fruits according to their color. Many citrus fruits are fully ripe when their skins are still green.

Most non-organic oranges have a film of wax on their skin; scrub the skin well to remove this wax before cooking, or buy unwaxed citrus fruit.

Try other Marmalade recipes ▶ ▶ ▶

Clementine and Whiskey Marmalade

3 medium jars

1¼ hours

9 months

Ingredients

2lb (900g) clementines, scrubbed and halved with seeds removed

juice of 2 large lemons

4 cups granulated sugar

1–2 tbsp whiskey (or brandy)

Put 1 or 2 small plates in the fridge to chill.

PREPARE THE CLEMENTINES

Chop the clementines in a food processor using the pulse button until they are shredded but not mushy.

Tip If you don't have a food processor, squeeze the juice from the fruit and shred the skins finely with a sharp knife.

SOFTEN THE RIND

Put the chopped fruit in a preserving pan or a large, heavy saucepan and add 3 cups of water. Turn the heat up high, bring to a boil, then reduce to a simmer and cook over low heat for 30 minutes or longer until the rind is soft.

BOIL TO A SET

Add the lemon juice and sugar to the pan. Keep the heat low and stir constantly until the sugar has dissolved and the sugar crystals are no longer visible. Turn the heat up high and bring to a boil. Keep the mixture in the pan at a rolling boil for 20–30 minutes, or until it thickens and reaches the setting point.

TEST FOR A SET

Take the pan off the heat and do a wrinkle test to see if the fruit mixture has set. Place a teaspoon of the mixture on a chilled plate, wait

for 60 seconds, and then push it with your finger. If it offers resistance and wrinkles as you push it, it has reached setting point. If the mixture hasn't set, bring it back to a rolling boil for another minute and test again.

CAN THE MARMALADE

Once the marmalade has set, stir in the whiskey (or brandy, if using) and leave the marmalade in the pan to cool for a few minutes.

Why? Allow the mixture to cool in the pan so that the fruit sinks from the surface and becomes more evenly distributed through the hot liquid.

Ladle the marmalade into warm, sterilized jars, leaving ¼in (5mm) headspace. Cover, seal with a two-part top, heat process for 5 minutes (see pp.116–121), and label. Once opened, keep refrigerated.

Pink Grapefruit Marmalade

4 large jars

2–2½ hours, plus time to steep

1 year

Ingredients

3 Florida pink grapefruit, weighing approx. 1lb 10oz (750g), washed

2 lemons, washed

approx. 6⅓ cups granulated sugar (see below)

Remember Before starting, always weigh the grapefruit whole and double it to calculate the quantity of sugar required. As a general rule, you will need double the weight of sugar to fruit.

Put 1 or 2 small plates in the fridge to chill.

PREPARE THE PEEL

Carefully peel the rind from the grapefruit and lemons and cut the rinds into very thin slivers.

Careful! Do not to leave any pith on the rinds, as it will make the marmalade bitter. Reserve any pith that you cut away, however, as you need to make use of its pectin content to achieve a good set.

Squeeze and reserve the juice from the lemons and grapefruit. After juicing, you are left with the thick pith "shells" of the grapefruit; reserve these.

Place any seeds and peeled off pieces of pith in a small bowl, add just enough cold water to cover, and set aside. Put the rind slivers, juice, and 4½ cups of water in a bowl, cover, and leave to stand overnight. Chop the grapefruit shells, tie them up in a piece of cheesecloth, and leave overnight.

SOFTEN THE RIND

Transfer the rind, juice, and water mixture to a preserving pan or large, heavy saucepan. Drain the water from the soaked seeds and pith and also add to the pan. Transfer the seeds and pith to the cheesecloth bag of grapefruit shells and also add to the pan. Simmer for 1½–2 hours, stirring

occasionally, or until the rind is very soft and the mixture has reduced by about half. Remove the cheesecloth bag, allow to cool slightly, and squeeze out any juice back into the pan. Discard the bags.

BOIL TO A SET

Add the sugar and, over low heat, keep stirring until it has dissolved. Then bring to a boil, and keep at a rolling boil for 20–30 minutes or until the mixture looks like it has thickened to setting point.

Take the pan off the heat. Do the wrinkle test to see if the mixture has set (see p.135). If the mixture hasn't set, bring it back to a rolling boil for another minute and test again.

CAN THE MARMALADE

When the marmalade has set, skim off any foam and leave in the pan for a few minutes, so the fruit can distribute itself more evenly. Stir the mixture gently to disperse the last of the rind and ladle into warm, sterilized jars, leaving ¼in (5mm) headspace. Cover, seal with a two-part top, heat process for 5 minutes (see pp.116–121), and label. Store in a cool, dark place. Once opened, keep refrigerated.

How to **Make Fruit Curd**

Fruit curds are one of the few preserves that include dairy produce—usually butter, but sometimes heavy cream—and eggs. Some recipes suggest cooking the ingredients from start to finish in one pan, but this increases the risk of overheating, and can make the mixture split. For greater control, cook the mix gently in a bowl in a pan of simmering water to give a superior, velvety result.

Maintain a gentle heat to retain freshness of the fruit

Melting and dissolving

Heat the fruit—use the juice, zest, and flesh of the citrus fruit if you want a robust curd, or just the juice if you prefer it smoother—with sugar and butter in a heavy-bottomed saucepan. Keep stirring until the butter has melted, the sugar has dissolved, and no gritty bits remain.

Cut the softened butter into small chunks before adding, so it melts easily in the pan

This cooking method diffuses the heat

Adding the eggs

Transfer the mixture to a large heatproof bowl set in or over a pan of barely simmering water. This gentle method of cooking keeps the curd from splitting. Pour the beaten eggs into the hot mixture through a fine-mesh strainer, stirring to avoid scrambling them.

Stir constantly to distribute the heat and prevent any one part getting too hot and "cooking" the eggs

The curd is ready if a trail remains when you push the curd across the spoon with your finger

Achieving the correct consistency

Cook the mixture gently for 20–40 minutes, making sure the water does not get too hot and cause the curd to boil and split. Keep stirring constantly. The curd is ready when it is thick enough to coat the back of a wooden spoon.

Can the curd as soon as it is cooked

Use sterilized equipment to transfer the curd from the pan to warm jars

Storing the curd

As soon as the curd is ready, remove it from the heat. Ladle while still hot into warm, sterilized jars, leaving ¼in (5mm) headspace—the curd will thicken slightly as it cools. Cover, seal with a two-part top, heat process for 5 minutes (see pp.116–121), and label. The curd can be stored for 1 month in the fridge.

Lemon Curd

The great pleasure in making curds is that such
simple ingredients result in a gorgeously tangy, creamy
spread. Like fruit butters and cheeses, the main
ingredients of the lemon curd are fruit and sugar, but
butter and eggs provide richness.

3 small jars **15 minutes** **1 month refrigerated**

Ingredients

11 tbsp unsalted butter, diced

2 cups granulated sugar

juice and zest of 4 organic lemons (juice about 1½ cups in total)

4 small or medium eggs, lightly beaten

Equipment

sharp knife

cutting board

grater

large heatproof bowl

large saucepan

wooden spoon

fine mesh strainer

jars with lids or cellophane covers and elastic bands

waxed paper discs

butter   **granulated sugar**

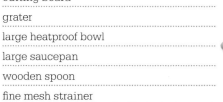

eggs   **organic lemons**   **sharp knife**

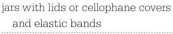

cutting board

grater

heatproof bowl   **saucepan**

wooden spoon   **fine mesh strainer**   **cellophane and waxed paper discs and elastic bands**   **jars**

MAKE FRUIT CURD

1 Prepare the zest by lightly grating the lemon rinds. Cut the lemons in half, squeeze out the juice, and reserve it. Put the lemon juice and zest in a pan and add the butter and sugar. Stir over low heat until the butter melts and the sugar dissolves.

Careful! Only grate the yellow part of the rind: the white pith beneath has a bitter taste.

Use a fine grater for the lemon skins so the zest almost dissolves into the curd

The simmering water should come just a little way up the bowl

2 Transfer the mixture to a heatproof bowl and set it in a pan of gently simmering water.

Help! If you're worried that the mixture might curdle, slow down the cooking stage by resting the bowl over a smaller saucepan so that the bottom of the bowl doesn't touch the simmering water; the mixture will cook by the heat of the steam instead.

3 Strain the beaten eggs into the mixture using a fine mesh strainer stirring constantly as you do so.

Careful! Keep your eye on the mixture: don't leave it unattended or you could quickly end up with split curd. Stirring the mix not only helps to keep the eggs from scrambling, but it also ensures that the mixture doesn't overheat at the bottom, or stick to the bowl.

Strain the beaten eggs to help keep lumps from forming and ensure a totally smooth finish

Stir the mixture constantly and ensure the heat remains low

The curd is set when it coats the back of a spoon and you can make a path with your finger

4 Cook the curd in the bowl very gently for 20–40 minutes; keep the water simmering and add more if necessary—don't boil the pan dry.

Help! Curd that starts to bubble and boil is in danger of splitting. Remove the bowl from the heat, set it in a bowl of iced water, and stir with a spoon until it cools. Return it to low heat and stir until it is the right consistency.

5 When the curd is ready, ladle into warm, sterilized jars, leaving ¼in (5mm) headspace. Cover, seal with a two-part top, heat process for 5 minutes (see pp.116–121), and label.

Remember The finished curd will continue to thicken as it cools, but if you think that the curd isn't quite thick enough when you test it, return it to the heat and cook it for a little longer.

Curds have a relatively short shelf life once opened, so can into small jars

How to store

Store the jars of curd in the refrigerator for up to 1 month. Keep each jar refrigerated once opened.

Did anything go wrong?

The curd is bubbling furiously. Pour the mix into a large, cold bowl and whisk vigorously to reduce the heat and rescue the mixture before it curdles. See also step 4 above.

The curd separated. The mixture cooked too quickly; the heat may have been too high, or unevenly distributed through the liquid. Next time try suspending the bowl over the water, keep the heat very low, and keep stirring to ensure the mixture remains at an even temperature.

Try other fruits

Any fruit with a slight sharpness makes a good curd, such as apricots, black currants, gooseberries, raspberries, limes, and grapefruit.

Try more Fruit Curd recipes ▶ ▶ ▶

Orange Curd

2 small jars **45–50 minutes** **1 month, refrigerated**

Ingredients

juice and rind of 2 large oranges, scrubbed to remove the wax, and finely grated

juice of 1 lemon, freshly squeezed

¾ cup granulated sugar

8 tbsp unsalted butter, diced

4 large egg yolks, lightly beaten

COMBINE THE INGREDIENTS

Put the orange rind and juice in a saucepan with the lemon juice and mix well. Add the sugar and butter to the pan and heat gently until the butter has melted and the sugar has dissolved. Transfer this mixture to a heatproof bowl and allow to cool slightly.

COOK THE CURD

Sit the heatproof bowl in a pan of very gently simmering water; the water should come only a short way up the side of the bowl.

Remember If preferred, you can cook over lower heat by resting the bowl over a smaller pan so that there is no contact between the water and the bottom of the bowl. The cooking time will be longer.

Strain the egg yolks and stir in. Cook the curd very gently, stirring constantly, for about 25–30 minutes or until the mixture has thickened and coats the back of a spoon. Test for a set with your finger: if you can draw a path through the curd on the back of the spoon, the curd is ready to can.

Careful! Be patient as the curd cooks. Stir constantly to ensure that heat is evenly distributed and do not allow it to boil because it will cause the mixture to separate.

CAN THE CURD

Remove the cooked curd from the heat and ladle into warm, sterilized jars, leaving ¼in (5mm) headspace. Cover, seal with a two-part top, heat process for 5 minutes (see pp.116–121), and label. Keep refrigerated and use within 1 month of making.

Serve orange curd as a tangy accompaniment to ice cream, or use it as a filling for cakes.

Remember Curds do not have a very long shelf life and must be stored in the fridge.

Raspberry Curd

2 small jars | **45–50 minutes** | **1 month, refrigerated**

Ingredients

9oz (250g) fresh raspberries

2 tbsp lemon juice, freshly squeezed

8 tbsp unsalted butter, diced

$2/3$ cup granulated sugar

4 large egg yolks and 1 large egg, lightly beaten

COMBINE THE INGREDIENTS

Process the raspberries in a food processor with the lemon juice, then strain the pulp to remove any seeds. Add the raspberry purée to a saucepan with the butter and sugar, and heat gently until the butter has melted and the sugar has dissolved. Transfer this mixture to a heatproof bowl and allow to cool slightly.

Tip To speed up the cooking, gently warm the granulated sugar in a low preheated oven for about 5 minutes before adding it to the purée.

COOK THE CURD

Place the heatproof bowl in a saucepan of very gently simmering water; the water should come only a short way up the side of the bowl.

Tip If preferred, you can cook over lower heat by resting the bowl over a smaller pan so that there is no contact between the water and the bottom of the bowl. The cooking time will be longer.

Strain the egg yolks and the egg into the bowl and cook over very low heat, stirring constantly, for about 25–30 minutes or until the mixture has thickened and coats the back of a spoon. If you can leave a trail with your finger, the curd is ready.

Help! If the curd starts to bubble or boil, act immediately to prevent it from curdling. Take the bowl off the heat. Either set it in a bowl of iced water and stir with a wooden spoon until the mixture cools, or tip the curd into a large cold bowl and whisk vigorously to reduce the temperature and distribute the heat more evenly.

CAN THE CURD

Remove the cooked curd from the heat and ladle into warm, sterilized jars, leaving ¼in (5mm) headspace. Cover, seal with a two-part top, heat process for 5 minutes (see pp.116–121), and label. Keep refrigerated and use within 1 month.

Serve raspberry curd as a topping for yogurt, or with whipped cream and meringues for an indulgent treat.

How to **Make Butter**

Traditionally butter—and indeed cheese—were methods of preserving surplus milk. Although storing milk is no longer such a problem, making your own butter can be a fun and satisfying experience. It's also surprisingly quick. You don't need special equipment—just an electric hand mixer or food processor, and about 30 minutes of your time.

.The mixture should look like yellow scrambled eggs as you near the end of whisking

..Grip the butterfat firmly and press hard to force out the liquid buttermilk

Make the butterfat

Butter is made from the fattiest parts of milk—or as we know it, cream. The first stage is to transform the cream into butterfat. Let stand for a couple of hours to sour. Then whisk for a few minutes to recreate the churning used in traditional butter-making.

Extract the buttermilk

Whisking separates the cream into solid butterfat and a liquid called buttermilk. All the buttermilk must be thoroughly squeezed out as it otherwise quickly turns sour and spoils the butter. Grooved butter pats are traditionally used but spatulas work well.

Use cold water to keep the butter from melting

Continue to rinse and squeeze the butter until the drained liquid runs clear

Push the butter down hard, or roll it tightly to expel air bubbles that can cause it to spoil

Wash the butter

As you squeeze out the buttermilk you can reserve it for soda bread and cake recipes or simply for drinking. Rinse the butterfat with cold water after each squeeze; when the water runs clear all the buttermilk will have been expelled and the fat is ready to mold.

Pack and shape the butter

Pack the butter firmly into a butter mold, adding salt between each layer to extend its shelf life. Alternatively, spread the butter in a thin layer and sprinkle it with salt. Mix together thoroughly, then shape the salted butter into a rectangular slab or a roll.

Salted and Unsalted Butter

Butter is quick and simple to make—and if you happen to have some spare cream in the fridge, it's a clever way to use it up. Add fresh herbs, crushed peppercorns, or minced garlic cloves to the finished butter and use it with fried fish or steak or to add flavor to sauces.

1lb 2oz (500g) | **Approx. 25 minutes** | **Up to 3 weeks if salted**

Ingredients

4 cups heavy cream, left at room temperature for 3 hours

1 tsp fine salt (optional)

Equipment

electric hand mixer or food processor

large bowl

strainer

wooden cutting board

wooden spatulas or butter pats

butter mold, ramekins, or waxed paper

heavy cream   **salt**

electric hand mixer

large bowl

wooden cutting board

strainer

butter mold

wooden spatulas

153

1 Pour the cream into a large, clean, sterilized bowl. Whisk the cream for a few minutes with an electric hand mixer until it is of a whipped consistency with soft peaks.

Tip If preferred, you can use a food processor to whisk the cream until it separates.

Use a low speed setting for the last minute of whisking

The mixture will look like a mass of small globules of fat

2 Keep whisking until the cream yellows, and resembles scrambled eggs. Whisk for another 2–3 minutes, or until it has split into buttermilk liquid and fat solids. Drain off the buttermilk.

Careful! When the mixture splits it will be difficult to continue whisking without the buttermilk spraying out of the bowl. The low speed setting gives you time to react—and stop—quickly.

3 Place the solid butterfat in a strainer and wash it under cold water before transferring it to a wooden board. Using wooden spatulas or butter pats, pick up clumps of butterfat and squeeze out the buttermilk.

Tip Soak your wooden utensils in iced water for about 30 seconds before you use them so they don't stick to the butter.

Avoid working the butterfat directly with your hands to prevent it from melting; use wooden utensils instead, which don't conduct heat

4 Continue squeezing the butterfat to expel buttermilk. Rinse the butter with cold water, then squeeze out more buttermilk, and repeat. The butter is ready when the water runs clear.

Cold water helps to keep the butter cool while you work

Why? The process of extracting all the buttermilk and washing the butterfat helps to extend the butter's shelf life, as buttermilk turns butter rancid.

5 Spoon or press the butterfat firmly into the butter mold or ramekins, or alternatively shape by hand into a roll or rectangle and wrap tightly in waxed paper. Store in the fridge and use within 7 days. If salting the butter, add the fat in layers and scatter salt over each layer.

Careful! Pack the butter in tightly to drive out air bubbles, which can spoil the butter.

How to store

Adding salt preserves the butter for 2–3 weeks in the fridge; alternatively freeze it for 2–3 months.

Did anything go wrong?

The cream doesn't seem to whip properly. You may be using homogenized cream. The homogenized cream will whip, but possibly not as well as you expect.

Try making flavored butters

Add herbs and spices to the butter along with the salt to create your own flavored butters. Try whole grain mustard with dried thyme and sage; finely chopped chives, dill, or mint; finely chopped parsley and lemon zest; or minced garlic. Store in the fridge for about 1 week, or roll into convenient portions and freeze for up to 3 months.

Try making Soft Cheese ▶ ▶ ▶

How to **Make Soft Cheese**

Historically, making soft cheese was regarded as another way to use up spare milk, and its alternative name—cottage cheese—reveals its humble origins. No special equipment or sophisticated processes are needed: just curdle some milk and strain off the watery by-product to make mild-tasting curds that can be enhanced with additional flavors.

Use a slotted spoon to skim off the curds

Do not allow the milk to boil: remove it from the heat as soon as it starts to simmer

Strain the curds overnight in a cheesecloth bag

Curdle the milk

Left to stand in a warm place, milk becomes more acidic, causing it to sour (or "curdle") and separate into curds and a watery whey. You can accelerate the process by gently warming milk in a saucepan then stirring in some lemon juice, which is naturally acidic.

Hang the curds

The soft cheese is made using the curds. Remove the curds from the liquid whey and allow them to dry out further by straining them overnight. The result is a soft cheese with a very mild taste, that is ready to flavor with herbs and spices.

Soft Cheese with Garlic and Herbs

Approx. 7oz (200g)   **1½–2 days**   **Up to 2 days**

Ingredients

4 cups whole milk

2 tbsp fresh lemon juice

½–1 clove garlic, finely chopped

2 tbsp freshly chopped mixed herbs,
    such as chives and parsley

sea salt and freshly ground black pepper

Special Equipment

cheesecloth

string

MAKE THE CHEESE
Pour the milk into a large, heavy-bottomed saucepan and heat gently until it is just below a boil. As soon as the milk begins to simmer, remove the pan from the heat.

Stir in the lemon juice to encourage curds to form, then leave undisturbed for 10 minutes to curdle.

Remember The lemon juice increases the acidity of the milk, and speeds up the curdling process.

DRAIN THE CHEESE
Line a strainer with cheesecloth and transfer the curds with a slotted spoon. Let strain for at least 30 minutes until most of the whey has drained off. Discard the whey.

Why? It is important to drain off all the liquid otherwise the cheese will be too soft and will not keep as long.

Pull the cheesecloth up around the curds and squeeze to remove excess liquid. Tie the ends of the cheesecloth with string and leave to strain overnight over a bowl in the refrigerator.

Tip Place the cheesecloth in a strainer over a large mixing bowl to catch the remaining drips of whey; alternatively, push a wooden spoon through the loops of the bag and suspend it over the bowl.

ADD THE FLAVORINGS
Unwrap the soft cheese from the cheesecloth and spread it out on a clean cutting board. Discard any whey that accumulated overnight.

Gently knead in the garlic, chives, and the rest of the seasoning until it is thoroughly mixed. Spoon the cheese into a clean jar, ramekins, or dishes and store in the fridge. Use within 2 days.

Tip The cheese will lose its texture and break down slightly after 2 days, but it's worth waiting for 24 hours before trying the cheese, to allow the flavors to mingle.

How to **Make Alcoholic Drinks**

Enjoying your own wine or hard cider need not be a distant dream. With some basic brewing equipment, careful preparation, and a little bit of patience you can make alcoholic drinks with delicious flavors from fruits, vegetables, and even flowers—simply add sugar and specialty wine or brewer's yeast and leave to ferment.

Equipment must be scrupulously clean to prevent contamination by rogue yeasts

Use unrefined cane sugar to boost the natural sugar content in the solution

Making the liquor juice

Wine and brewer's yeasts contain specially selected microbes that break down or "feed on" very sugary acidic liquor and convert it to alcohol. It is usually necessary to add extra sugar to fruit juices to supplement their natural sugar content. Mash the fruit according to the recipe and strain the pulp with the help of a sterilized jelly bag, cheesecloth, or cheesecloth-lined strainer set over a sterilized bowl. If you are making cider, add the sugar directly to the strained juice. If you are making wine, dissolve the sugar in a bowl of hot water and allow the mixture to cool before adding it to the prepared fruit.

Leave room at the top for the bubbly "head" that forms when yeast is added

Always use sterilized equipment to avoid complications like mold developing

Add more water in the airlock during the fermentation process if necessary

Carbon dioxide passes out as bubbles rising through the airlock

Airlock prevents air and foreign bodies from contaminating the juice

Ferment the liquor

Pour the juice through a sterilized funnel into a sterilized demijohn, leaving a reasonable head space at the top. Add the yeast. Specialty yeasts ensure consistent, predictable results and eliminate unwanted wild yeasts, such as those that naturally occur on grape skins.

Fit an airlock

Once fermentation is underway, fit an airlock to the demijohn and pour a little water into it to allow carbon dioxide to escape as bubbles while the juice ferments. The bubbles cease once fermentation is complete; the yeast eventually dies off and collects as clumps of sediment at the bottom of the demijohn.

Hard Cider

Cider is made from fermented apple juice. You can use any type of apple, including windfalls. Generally, the sharper the variety, the drier the cider. Choose a sweeter variety if you prefer a sweet cider, or use one-third each of bittersweet, sweet, and tart apples for a delicious mix.

14 cups   **3 months**   **6 months**

apples

champagne
yeast

cane sugar

Ingredients

7–8lb (3.5kg) apples, or
   14 cups apple juice

⅛oz (5g) champagne yeast

½ cup unrefined cane sugar

jelly bag

Equipment

food processor or electric fruit juicer

jelly bag or cheesecloth-lined strainer

large bowl

hydrometer (to measure the specific
   gravity of liquids)

measuring cup

demijohn and siphon

long-spouted funnel

cotton balls

airlock and rubber bung

glass bottles

corks and a corker

food processor

bowl

demijohn
and
siphon

hydrometer

corks

measuring cup

long-
spouted
funnel

cotton balls

airlock

bottles

1 Check that the apples are in good condition and cut away any bruised parts. Place the apples in the freezer and leave them overnight. Allow the apples to thaw thoroughly, then process them in a food processor.

Why? Freezing the apples softens them by breaking down their fibrous walls.

Reduce the thawed apples to a pulp

Strain the pulp in small batches if necessary

2 Strain the pulp through a jelly bag or clean, cheesecloth-lined strainer set over a bowl until you have collected 14 cups of juice. Use a hydrometer to measure the gravity of the juice. It should read between 1,035 and 1,050.

Help! If the gravity is not within range, gradually dilute the juice with water until it is.

3 Add the sugar to the juice and keep stirring until it is dissolved. Using a sterilized funnel, pour the juice into a sterilized demijohn.

Remember Be scrupulous about sterilizing all your brewing equipment to eliminate unwanted contaminants. This prevents airborne microorganisms from contaminating the brew and causing it to deteriorate.

Pour carefully: control the flow to minimize splashing and avoid aerating the liquor.

Fill the demijohn to the shoulder to leave room for the liquor to froth as it ferments

Adding yeast initiates the fermentation process

4 Add the yeast and seal the demijohn with cotton balls. Leave at room temperature for 2 days. When the frothing reduces, replace the cotton balls with a sterilized airlock and pour water into it. Leave for at least 2 weeks or until the airlock stops bubbling.

Why? Cotton balls allow carbon dioxide to escape more easily in the vigorous stage of fermentation, and exclude microorganisms.

5 Siphon the cider into bottles. The bottle must be below the level of the liquid in the demijohn. Put one end of the siphon in the demijohn, suck it like a straw to fill it with cider, and swiftly insert the tube into the bottle. Lift each bottle as it fills to control the flow and move the tube to the next bottle.

Careful! Make sure fermentation is complete before you bottle the cider, or the bottles may explode.

Allow ³⁄₄in (2cm) of head space in case of expansion

How to seal and store

To seal, put a cork in the corker, place over the bottle, and pull the lever to insert the cork fully.

Leave cider for about 3 months in a dark place at room temperature (sunlight can cause it to spoil).

Store corked bottles sideways so the corks keep moist—dry corks shrink and let in too much air, which spoils the cider. Cider is best consumed within 6 months.

Did anything go wrong?

If your cider doesn't taste right, you may have put the demijohn in too warm or too cold a place during fermentation, or you may not have sterilized your equipment properly. Alternatively, you may have stored the corked bottles upright and allowed the air in, spoiling the brew.

Your cider may also not taste right if you used baker's yeast instead of a specialty yeast. Always check the recipe and use the correct ingredients.

Try more Alcoholic Drink recipes ▶ ▶ ▶

Greengage Wine

**1 gallon
(4.5 liters)**   **8 months**   **2 years**

Ingredients

4½lb (2kg) greengage plums, washed

juice of 1 lemon

1 tsp pectolase (a pectolytic enzyme)

1 tsp wine yeast

6 cups unrefined cane sugar

Special Equipment

fermenting bin or large bucket

potato masher

cheesecloth

PREPARE THE FRUIT

Put the greengages in the freezer overnight. This starts to break down the pectin that can otherwise turn the wine cloudy. Defrost thoroughly.

Pit the fruit, add it to the fermenting bin, and mash it with a potato masher. Add the lemon juice and pour in 12 cups of boiling water. Let cool. Add the pectolase, which removes the remaining pectin from the juice. Cover and leave for 24 hours at room temperature.

Careful! Room temperature ranges from 59–77°F (15–25°C); if your room is hotter or colder than this, it will affect the result, so try to improve the conditions or find a different place to make the wine.

ADD THE YEAST

Add the yeast to the fruit mixture, cover, and leave for 4–5 days in the dark at room temperature.

Pour the fruit mixture into cheesecloth (fit the cheesecloth inside a sterilized strainer if required) set over a sterilized bowl and collect the juice.

ADD THE SUGAR

Put the sugar into a large bowl. Pour in enough hot water to cover the sugar and stir until it has dissolved—add more hot water if you need to, and continue stirring until the sugar crystals are no longer visible. Cool, then stir the liquid into the juice.

Tip If you are using very ripe fruit, the wine may be a little sweet if you use the recommended quantity of sugar. For a drier wine, use a little less sugar.

LEAVE TO FERMENT

Using a sterilized funnel, transfer the sugary juice into a sterilized demijohn, then fit a sterilized airlock. Pour a little water into the airlock and then leave the liquid to ferment for 2 months at room temperature.

BOTTLE THE WINE

Check the airlock regularly. When there are no bubbles in the airlock, transfer the wine into sterilized bottles using a sterilized siphon. Leave ¾in (2cm) of space at the top of each bottle. Seal, label, and store in a cool, dark place for 6 months before opening.

Why? Leave space at the top in case temperatures fluctuate and the wine expands. The small amount of air at the top of the bottle also allows the wine to age without becoming oxidized.

Elderflower Champagne

1 gallon
(4.5 liters)   **2 weeks**   **3 months**

Ingredients

5 cups unrefined cane sugar

8 large elderflower heads

2 lemons, sliced

juice of 2 lemons

¼ cup white wine vinegar

Special Equipment

2 fermenting bins or large buckets

cheesecloth

DISSOLVE THE SUGAR

Pour the sugar into a fermenting bin and add 28 cups of boiling water. Cover and let cool.

PREPARE THE FLOWERS

Gently shake the flower heads to remove any insects. Add the flower heads to the sugar solution.

Why? The elderflowers not only flavor the drink, but the wild yeasts that are naturally present in the flowers are used for fermentation. No additional yeast is added so the champagne is only mildly alcoholic—if at all.

Add the lemon juice, lemon slices, and vinegar, cover with a clean cloth, and leave for 24 hours.

STRAIN THE LIQUID

Pour the liquid through a fine strainer or cheesecloth into a sterilized bucket.

Tip Squeeze the flower heads as you strain the liquid to release the maximum amount of flavor.

BOTTLE THE WINE

Transfer the liquid into sterilized bottles using a sterilized long-necked funnel, leaving ¾in (2cm) of space at the top of each bottle. Seal, label, and store the bottles in a cool, dark place for 10–14 days.

Remember Closely monitor wine stored in plastic bottles. Keep the bottles in a dark place to keep the plastic from degrading. Check the bottles every day and release a little air to prevent them from swelling.

How to **Dry- and Wet-cure Fish**

Dry-curing white and oily fish with fine sea salt not only prolongs its shelf life by a few days, but also helps to develop its flavor and firm its texture, making it taste as good as cooked. Wet-curing fish by pickling it in vinegar and brine also adds richness and flavor. The vinegar acts in a similar way to heat, changing the structure of the fish's protein and effectively "cooking" it.

Dry-curing the fish

If you are arranging small fish in layers, sprinkle salt over each layer.

COVERING THE FISH IN A "CURE"

Put the fish in a shallow dish and sprinkle with a layer of fine sea salt to draw out moisture, which inhibits the growth of microbes. Cover with plastic wrap and let cure in the fridge as stated in the recipe. Place a weight on top to remove more liquid and speed up the process.

Dry the fish carefully using paper towels

DRYING THE FISH

Turn the fish every 12 hours. Moisture collects in the dish as the fillets cure; drain the liquid to keep the fish from reabsorbing it. Cured fillets should be firm in texture and easy to slice. Pat dry with paper towels to remove any excess salt and store for up to 2 days in the fridge.

Wet-curing the fish

Allow the fish to absorb the brine for 2–3 hours

Keep the fish submerged in the vinegar

You can add additional flavorings

SOFTENING THE FISH WITH BRINE
Soak the fish fillets in brine for a few hours, then drain and dry with paper towels. The brine penetrates the fish, inhibiting the growth of bacteria and drawing out moisture.

Leave the spices to steep in the vinegar

MAKING PICKLING VINEGAR
Slowly bring the vinegar, sugar, and spices to a boil in a stainless-steel pan. Simmer for 2 minutes and let cool. A plain vinegar can also be used, but pickling vinegar adds flavor.

PICKLING IN THE VINEGAR
Place the fish in a sterilized jar and cover with vinegar. The longer the fish is pickled, the more mature its flavor. As vinegar is a preservative, the fish keeps for longer than dry-cured fillets.

Gravalax

Fresh fish is a delicate food, so it requires gentle
preserving methods to improve its flavor and taste.
This traditional Scandinavian method of salting salmon
to gradually alter its natural qualities is easy to try
using ordinary kitchen equipment.

2¼lb (1kg) | **2 days** | **3–4 days (refrigerator); 2 months (frozen)**

Ingredients

⅓ cup granulated sugar or light brown sugar (optional; see step 1)

1oz (30g) dill, chopped

1 tbsp lemon juice

¼ cup fine sea salt

1 tsp freshly ground black pepper

2 x 1lb 2oz (500g) thick salmon fillets

Equipment

small bowl

clean tray, large enough to accommodate the salmon fillets

plastic wrap

ladle or large spoon

paper towels

sharp knife

wooden cutting board

granulated sugar

dill

lemon juice

sea salt

black pepper

salmon

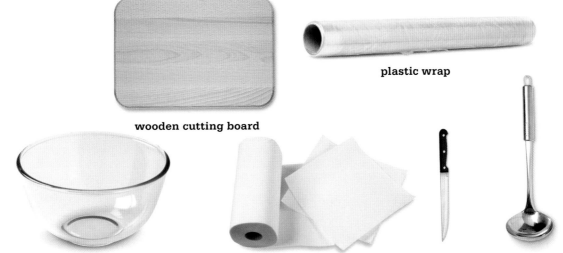

wooden cutting board

plastic wrap

small bowl

paper towels

sharp knife

ladle

1 Get your fishmonger to prepare two matching fillets of salmon, one from either side of the same fish, removing all the bones in the process. Make the dry-cure mix: put the sugar, dill, lemon juice, salt, and pepper in a small bowl and combine thoroughly.

Tip Use light brown sugar instead of granulated sugar if you want a slightly deeper, richer flavor, and darker color.

Spread the curing mix with your fingers and rub it into the flesh

2 Lay one of the salmon fillets skin-side down in the tray. Spread the curing mix evenly over the flesh.

Careful! Check for any stray bones by running your finger along the fillets before you add the cure.

3 Place the second salmon fillet on top of the first, flesh-side down. Wrap the fillets tightly in plastic wrap, leaving the head and tail ends open so liquid runs out. Place a weight on top and leave to cure in the fridge for 48 hours.

Tip Compressing the fillets helps to squeeze moisture out. Place a plate or board on top of the fish and weigh it down with cans.

Lay one fillet carefully over the other to cover the curing mix completely

4 Turn the wrapped fish every 12 hours to compress each fillet thoroughly, and drain off the moisture drawn out of the fillets. After 48 hours, remove the plastic wrap, pat dry with paper towels, and slice with a sharp knife.

Remember The cured fish will be a bit smaller and much firmer than the original fillets.

Remove the liquid to ensure the fillets firm up

How to store

Refrigerate the sliced gravalax and eat it within 3–4 days. Alternatively, you can freeze it for up to 2 months.

Did anything go wrong?

The fish isn't firm enough to slice. It may still contain too much moisture. Continue curing for up to 5 days; use a heavier weight. Do not eat fish if you think it has spoiled, or fish that smells rancid.

Try other fish

Other fish to dry-cure include very fresh trout, mackerel, and halibut. Always use the freshest fish you can find.

If you use wild salmon, freeze it for at least 24 hours and leave to thaw in the fridge before dry-curing. Freezing kills the parasites that may be found in wild fish.

Try more Cured Fish recipes ▶ ▶ ▶

Rollmops

1 medium jar

3–4 days

1 month, refrigerated

Ingredients

6–8 very fresh herring fillets, descaled and trimmed, with any visible bones removed

1 red onion, finely sliced

6–8 pickled gherkins

For the brine

¼ cup sea salt per 2 cups of cold water

For the spiced vinegar

2 cups cider or white wine vinegar

1 tbsp light brown sugar

6 black peppercorns

6 allspice berries

1 blade of mace

3 bay leaves

1 dried chile

Special Equipment

cocktail sticks

SOAK IN BRINE

Arrange the herring fillets in a large, shallow glass dish and pour the brine over the top to cover them completely. Leave to soak for 2–3 hours. Drain the brine and dry each fillet with paper towels.

Help! The amount of brine required depends on the number and size of the fillets as well as the size of the dish. To work out approximate quantities, fill the dish with water to about the half-way point and pour into a large measuring cup. You can then calculate how much salt to dissolve in the water.

MAKE THE SPICED VINEGAR

Put all the ingredients for the spiced vinegar in a stainless-steel saucepan and bring slowly to a boil. Simmer for 1–2 minutes, then set aside to cool.

ROLL THE FILLETS

Lay out the fillets skin-side down on a clean cutting board. Place an onion slice and a gherkin on the tail-end of a fillet and roll it up. Secure with a cocktail stick. Repeat with the rest of the fillets.

PACK THE JAR

Put the rollmops in a sterilized jar and pour in the cold spiced vinegar—including the spices—so that it covers the fish completely. Add extra vinegar, if needed. Seal and store in the fridge for 3–4 days to mature.

Remember Always keep the fish submerged in the vinegar to ensure they don't spoil.

Quick Salted Herrings

1 small jar **1–3 days if marinating** **1–2 weeks**

Ingredients

2 very fresh herring fillets, boned, with head, excess skin, and fins removed

small slivers of lemon peel (optional)

olive oil, to cover (if marinating)

For the cure mix

2 tsp fine sea salt

2 tsp granulated sugar

1 tsp brandy

freshly ground black pepper

2 tsp fresh dill, chopped

CURE THE FILLETS

In a small bowl, combine the ingredients for the cure mix.

Place the largest fillet skin-side down on a clean plate. Spread the cure over the fillet, making sure that the flesh is completely covered. Place the second fillet on top of the first, skin-side up.

Wrap the fillet sandwich in plastic wrap, weigh it down with a heavy weight, and leave for 24 hours in the fridge to cure. Leave the head and tail ends of the plastic wrap open so that liquid can run out of the package when you turn the fillets.

Why? Wrapping the fillets in plastic wrap holds the sandwich together and ensures that the cure remains in contact with the flesh throughout the process, drawing out moisture and adding flavor.

Turn the fillets after 12 hours and drain off any liquid. After 24 hours, the fillets should be firm and ready to eat. Remove the plastic wrap, drain, and pat dry with paper towels.

The fillets can be refrigerated for up to 1 week: transfer them to a clean plate, cover with plastic wrap, and store in the fridge. For a deeper flavor (and slightly longer shelf life of up to 2 weeks) try marinating the fillets in oil.

MARINATE THE FILLETS

Slice the fillets thinly and remove the skins. Place the fillets in a sterilized jar, add the lemon peel (if required), and pour in enough oil to cover the slivers of fillet completely. Leave in the fridge for 48 hours to mature before eating.

How to **Wet- and Dry-cure Meat**

Curing meat is an age-old preserving technique. Originally a cold cellar was required to achieve the right results, but these days a fridge makes the process more convenient. It's worthwhile preserving meat yourself: there's nothing like the taste of home-cured food, and it is an excellent way to flavor and extend the shelf life of cheaper cuts of meat.

Wet-cure method

...... Make sure the brine completely covers the meat—if necessary use a clean glass paperweight or plate to weigh down the meat

Choose a container large enough to hold the meat and its cure, and make sure it fits on the bottom shelf of the fridge ......

Careful! Both brining and dry-curing create an air-free environment that prevents the growth of microorganisms. It is important to check that your fridge is cold enough to ensure the curing process is safe. The temperature should read 41°F (5°C), or slightly below.

THE BRINING PROCESS

To cure, the raw meat must sit in a salty solution—sometimes for up to 25 days. Use a plastic container with an airtight lid, and make sure that the meat will be submerged throughout the process. Secure the lid tightly and place it in the fridge for the required time.

Dry-cure method

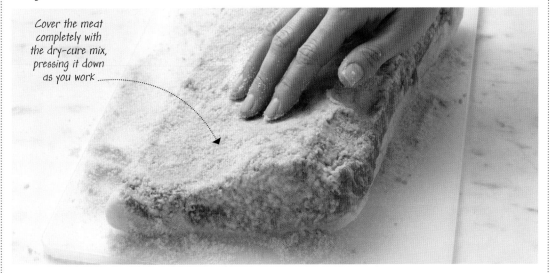

Cover the meat completely with the dry-cure mix, pressing it down as you work

APPLYING THE DRY-CURE MIX

Salting meat not only draws out moisture, but is also an opportunity to add flavor. To apply the dry-cure mix, place the meat skin-side down on a clean cutting board. Use your fingers to spread the cure evenly over the flesh and fat, rubbing it into all the crevices.

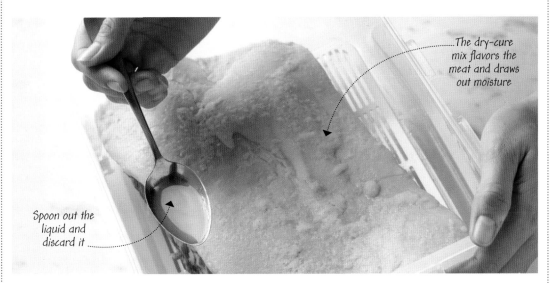

The dry-cure mix flavors the meat and draws out moisture

Spoon out the liquid and discard it

ALLOWING THE MEAT TO MATURE

Place the cured meat on a drip tray in a plastic container, seal with an airtight lid, and store in the fridge for the required length of time to cure properly and allow the flavors to mature. Check the meat regularly and drain off any watery liquid that collects under the tray.

Dry-cured Bacon

Dry-curing is a simple process, and a popular starting point for beginners. It's also the best way to prepare delicious breakfast bacon. Use fresh, good-quality pork to ensure the tastiest results.

4½lb (2kg)   **8–12 days**   **2–3 months**

Ingredients

4½lb (2kg) boneless pork loin, skin on (preferably)

For the dry-cure mix

¼ cup curing salt

2 tbsp light brown sugar

1 rounded tsp citric or ascorbic acid (vitamin C powder)

Equipment

mixing bowl

cutting board

large plastic container with lid and drip tray or rack in the bottom

spoon

sharp knife

paper towels

cheesecloth

curing salt

boneless pork loin

light brown sugar   **ascorbic acid**   **mixing bowl**

cutting board

spoon

sharp knife

plastic container with drip tray   **paper towels**   **cheesecloth**

1 Combine the ingredients for the dry-cure mix in a bowl. Lay the raw meat on a clean cutting board, skin-side down, and cover it with the cure mix.

Remember Always wash your hands before and after handling raw meat.

Rub the cure into all the exposed flesh including both ends

Don't forget to rub some of the curing mix into the skin

2 Transfer the meat to a large plastic container with a drip tray in the bottom and an airtight lid. Seal the container and place it on the bottom shelf of the fridge for 4–5 days.

Careful! It is important to be fastidious about hygiene when dealing with raw pork. Do not allow any other food in the fridge to come into contact with it.

3 Check the loin at regular intervals and drain off the watery liquid that collects below the drip tray. Rub any salty sediment back into the meat.

Why? If you allow the meat to reabsorb the curing juices, it will take longer for the meat to dry at the end of the process.

Use a spoon to drain the liquid

A uniformly pink color indicates that the cure has reached the center of the pork

4 To check that the bacon is sufficiently cured, cut a thin slice from one end. It should be pink across the length of the slice.

Help! If you see a gray patch in the center of the slice, make up half quantities of the curing mix and reapply to the loin. Put the meat back into the container, seal, and return it to the fridge for another 24 hours.

5 Rinse the pork in cold water and dry with paper towels. Wrap in clean cheesecloth, place back in its container, and refrigerate uncovered—away from other food—for another 4–5 days.

Why? Leaving the bacon in the fridge uncovered allows it to dry out a little more. The meat will darken and become firmer to the touch. Check it's ready to eat by frying and tasting a sample slice.

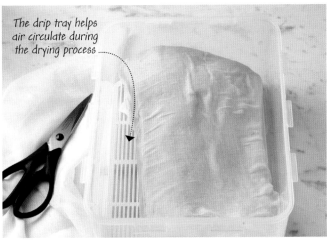

The drip tray helps air circulate during the drying process

How to store

Wrap the bacon in waxed paper and store in the fridge for up to 10 days, cutting off slices as and when desired. Though cured, the meat cannot be eaten raw and must be cooked.

Alternatively, divide the meat into conveniently-sized portions and freeze for 2–3 months.

Did anything go wrong?

The bacon tastes too salty after curing. Soak the loin in cold water in the fridge for 24 hours. Pat dry with paper towels and wrap in cheesecloth. Refrigerate uncovered for another 3–4 days.

The meat has gone moldy. If there is green or black mold on the cured meat, the storage atmosphere may have been too damp and warm. Discard the meat; do not eat.

Try more meat preserves ▶ ▶ ▶

Wet-cured Ham

There are many ways to cure pork into ham, but this basic
method gives the meat a mild, sweet flavor. The sugar is
an important ingredient in the cure mix as it helps to
soften the meat, which might otherwise become
toughened by the high salt content.

5½lb
(2.5kg)

 1 month

 4–5 days,
cooked

**fresh ham
with skin on**

**curing
salt**

**light
brown sugar**

Ingredients

5½lb (2.5kg) fresh ham with skin on

For the cure mix

3 cups curing salt

2 tbsp light brown sugar

1 tbsp ascorbic acid
  (vitamin C powder)

For cooking and finishing the ham

1 cup hard cider

1 dried bay leaf

12 black peppercorns

6 cloves

**ascorbic
acid**

cider

bay leaf

**black
peppercorns**

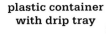

cloves

Equipment

large plastic container with lid and
  drip tray or rack in the bottom

drip tray or rack

baking sheet

kitchen string

cheesecloth

large saucepan

**plastic container
with drip tray**

**kitchen
string**

baking sheet

cheesecloth

large saucepan

1 Put 25 cups of water in a large sterilized plastic container with a lid. Add all the curing ingredients and stir the solution well until everything has dissolved.

Help! The cure will fizz and may smoke a little—don't worry, this is perfectly normal.

Sprinkling the ingredients on to the water will help them to dissolve faster

2 Place the meat in the container and make sure that it is completely submerged in the brine. Seal the container and refrigerate the pork for 25 days.

Tip If necessary, use a clean plate or paperweight to weigh down the pork. Check regularly to ensure that the meat remains submerged throughout the curing time.

Check that the cure ingredients are fully dissolved before adding the pork

3 Lift the meat out of the brine and pat dry with paper towels. Place it on a rack or drip tray set over a baking sheet, truss into a round with kitchen string, wrap the meat in cheesecloth, and refrigerate for 3–4 days.

Why? The drip tray will catch the moisture dripping from the pork as it dries out, and also allows air to circulate.

The pork will still look like raw meat after brining

4 To cook, soak the ham in cold water for 1 hour. Bring a large saucepan of water to a boil, add the cider, seasonings, and ham, then bring back to a boil. Cover and barely simmer over low heat for 3–3½ hours.

Remember The ham is not ready to eat until it has been properly cooked.

The aromatic spices and cider enhance the flavor of the ham as it cooks ....

How to store

Boiled ham may be stored in the fridge for 4–5 days. Alternatively, divide into convenient portions and freeze for 2–3 months.

Honey roast ham is finished in the oven with a sweet glaze: mix 2 level tablespoons each of maple syrup, honey, and mustard, or use 5 tablespoons of marmalade. Spread the glaze over the ham. Roast in a hot oven (400°F/ 200°C) for 30–40 minutes. Cold roast ham keeps in the fridge for up to 5 days.

Uncooked cured meat may be refrigerated for up to 3 days, or frozen for 1–2 months.

Did anything go wrong?

The pork smells unpleasant. Discard the meat; do not eat it.

The brine has changed consistency. The curing mix didn't contain enough salt, or the storage temperature was too high. Redo the whole process.

White salt burns appear on the cured meat. The salt solution was too strong.

The cured meat has green or black mold. Your salt solution was too weak, and the meat wasn't cured properly. Discard the meat.

Try more meat preserves ▶ ▶ ▶

How to **Pot Meats**

Succulent potted meats make delicious, inexpensive snacks—simply serve with toast. Potting is a great way to preserve cheap cuts, such as beef shank or pork belly, and using this technique you can extend the life of leftovers, too. Shred the cooked meat (or process to a paste), pot it, then seal with an airtight layer of clarified butter or lard.

Pack the meat

Cook the meat until tender and almost falling apart; reserve the juices. Purée the meat in a food processor to make a smooth paste, or shred by hand for a more coarse-textured preserve. Allow it to cool, then pack into a warm sterilized jar, add any reserved juices, and level the top.

Leave at least ½in (1cm) for the layer of fat and firmly press in the meat

Strain with a cheesecloth-lined strainer to remove any white, milky sediment

The butter cools into a ½in (1cm) solid layer, blocking off bacteria

Seal the pot

A layer of fat creates an airtight seal that excludes airborne microbes but keeps the meat moist. Clarified butter (from which water and milk solids are removed) has a good shelf life, preserving the meat longer. Melt the butter in a pan over low heat. Let it foam for a few seconds then remove from the heat, skim off the froth, and allow to cool slightly. Strain the melted butter into a bowl. Pour over the surface of the meat.

Potted Beef

Approx. 1lb 2oz (500g)

5–5½ hours

1 month, refrigerated

Ingredients

2lb (900g) beef osso bucco, trimmed and diced

2 cups beef stock

1¼ cups red wine

1 small onion, peeled and quartered

2 garlic cloves, peeled

few fresh bay leaves

few sprigs of thyme

pinch of ground mace

½ tsp mustard powder

24 tbsp unsalted butter, softened

salt and freshly ground black pepper

Special Equipment

ovenproof Dutch oven

food processor

cheesecloth

ramekins or small serving dishes

Preheat the oven to 325°F (160°C).

COOK THE BEEF

Place the beef in a large Dutch oven, pour in the stock and red wine, and scatter with the onion, garlic, bay leaves, and thyme. Bring to a simmer and then cover and cook in the oven for 2½–3 hours, until very tender.

Tip If you prefer, you can simmer the beef on the stove for the same length of time until tender.

CHOP THE MEAT

Drain the liquid and remove the onion, garlic, and herbs. Transfer the cooked meat to a food processor, add the mace, mustard, and 8 tbsp of the softened butter, and process, or chop by hand if preferred, until smooth or slightly textured.

POT THE BEEF

Season the meat mixture liberally. Spoon the mixture into ramekins or small serving dishes and chill for 2 hours.

SEAL THE BEEF

Melt the remaining butter in a saucepan, skim off the foam, and cool slightly. Pour the melted butter through a cheesecloth-lined strainer, discarding the milky sediment left at the bottom of the pan, and cool slightly.

Pour the clarified butter over the tops of the dishes to form a layer about ½in (1cm) thick. Chill until the butter has set, then garnish with bay leaves and cranberries if you like.

Pork Rillettes

1 small jar   **2 days**   **1 month, refrigerated**

Ingredients

1 tbsp rosemary, chopped

1 large garlic clove, crushed

¼ tsp cloves, ground

2 tsp sea salt

black pepper, freshly ground

1lb 2oz (500g) piece of bone-in pork belly

1 bay leaf

¼ cup lard, if needed

Special Equipment

small bowl

large plastic container with lid

casserole dish

cooking foil

small saucepan

cutting board

small preserving jar

MAKE THE RUB

In a small bowl, mix together the rosemary, garlic, cloves, salt, and black pepper. Place the meat in a large container with a sealable lid and, using your hands, cover it in the rub.

Tip Cover the meat completely in the rub, using your fingers to work it thoroughly into the skin and meat.

Seal the container and store the meat in the fridge for 24 hours.

COOK THE MEAT

Preheat the oven to 300°F (150°C).

Transfer the meat to a casserole dish, and add the bay leaf and 1 cup boiling water. Cover the dish tightly with cooking foil, put the lid on, and cook in the low oven for 3 hours until the meat is really tender and almost falls off the bone.

Careful! The meat needs to stay moist as it cooks, so check it after 1½ hours of cooking time. If the water has evaporated, add a little more water—a couple of tablespoonfuls should be enough.

Take the casserole out of the oven and drain off and reserve the melted fat, which will have collected in a layer above the juices. Transfer the pork and its juices into a strainer set over a bowl, cover, and allow to cool. If there is lots of fat in the juices, spoon it off and add it to the reserved fat. Reserve the juices, too.

PACK THE JAR

Once the pork is cold, remove the rind and bones and discard them, and put the pork on a cutting board.

Shred the meat—use two forks back to back to pull it apart—and pack it into a sterilized jar. Add the reserved juices.

In a small saucepan, melt the reserved fat over low heat. Pour it over the meat so that it covers the meat completely.

Tip If there isn't enough fat to cover the surface, melt some lard and add that to the jar.

Seal the jar, label, and, once cooled, refrigerate for up to 1 month.

Remember The pork rillettes keep for up to 2 days in the fridge after the jar is opened.

Duck Confit

4 servings

2¾ hours

2 weeks, refrigerated

Ingredients

2 tbsp sea salt

8 black peppercorns, lightly crushed

2 large garlic cloves, crushed

¼ tsp ground allspice

1 tsp dried thyme

2 bay leaves, torn into pieces

4 duck legs

12oz (350g) goose or duck fat

a little lard, if needed

Special Equipment

small bowl

large plastic container with lid

medium casserole dish

frying pan (to reheat for serving)

MAKE THE RUB

In a small bowl, combine the salt, peppercorns, garlic, allspice, thyme, and bay leaves. Place the duck legs in a large container with a sealable lid and, using your hands, cover them in the rub.

Seal the container and store the duck legs in the fridge for 24 hours.

COOK THE MEAT

Preheat the oven to 300°F (150°C).

Rinse the duck legs thoroughly with cold water and pat dry with paper towels.

Why? Rinsing is important to prevent the finished dish from tasting too salty—but the flavors from the rub are retained by the flesh.

Place the duck in a medium-sized flameproof casserole dish. Add the goose or duck fat and heat over low heat until the fat has melted—for about 10 minutes.

Cover the dish with a lid and cook in the low oven for 2½ hours until the meat is really tender.

Take the meat out of the oven and set aside until fairly cool. Transfer to a container with a sealable lid and pour the fat over the top to cover the meat completely; if necessary, add the extra lard. Seal, allow to cool, and store in the fridge.

SERVING THE CONFIT

Remove the duck from the container and scrape off the fat.

Tip Reserve the fat for the future: you can store it in the fridge and use it again for making confit up to 3 times.

Heat a large, heavy-bottomed frying pan and cook the duck for about 5 minutes on each side. Cook the duck skin-side down, first over high heat; then, reduce the heat, turn the duck over, and cook until piping hot all the way through.

Index

Acknowledgments

Photographic Credits

Dorling Kindersley would like to thank **Peter Anderson** and **Dave King** for new photography. All images © Dorling Kindersley. For further information see www.dkimages.com

Publisher's Acknowledgments

Many people helped in the making of this book. Dorling Kindersley would like to thank:

In the UK
Design assistance Vicky Read
Editorial assistance Annelise Evans, Helen Fewster, Holly Kyte
DK Images Claire Bowers, Freddie Marriage, Emma Shepherd, Romaine Werblow
Indexer Chris Bernstein

In India
Senior Editor Garima Sharma
Senior Art Editors Ranjita Bhattacharji, Ivy Roy
Design assistance Devan Das, Prashant Kumar, Ankita Mukherjee, Anamica Roy, Suzena Sengupta
Editor Arani Sinha
Editorial assistance Suefa Lee, Swati Mittal
DTP Designers Rajesh Singh Adhikari, Sourabh Chhallaria, Arjinder Singh
CTS/DTP Manager Sunil Sharma